The
9
Keys

Riz Mirza

Words

This beautiful and heartfelt offering from Riz Mirza contains amazing, life-changing words of wisdom from Red Eagle! Every page is filled with easy-to-understand, yet powerful guidance to help you achieve self-mastery, inner peace, love, joy, perfect health and fulfillment! What could be more important? I believe these are the deepest longings of our hearts and soul. Thank you, Riz and Red Eagle for this valuable information!

-Pamala Oslie, author of *Infinite You*

The 9 Keys will put you on the path to the most magical life ever!

-Marla Martenson, award-winning author of *The Buddha Made Me Do It*

"The Guides' messages are profound and deep and definitely life-changing."

-Marie-Ange Faugérolas, best selling author of *Angels*

ISBN: 9781711278162
Messages From the Spirit Guides to
Unlock Your Life

Photographer
Samia Kyriakis of Riz Mirza
Photography Book Cover Photograph
by Jeff Nissan

Assembly, Edit & Book Design Oriah Mirza
First printing edition 2019

Red Eagle Universal LLC

https://www.rizmirza.com/

Dedication

To Oriah without whom none of this would
be possible. I love you. And Alex Murray
my teacher in NYC, one of the greatest
psychics and Trance Channels of all time.
Thank you Alex.

Contents

Acknowledgments

To my stepdaughter Alexandria, my healer cat Baby Spice, my sidekick in psychic antics Erika Merriweather my book guru Julie McCarron, my brother Doug Curtis, my cosmic sister Joddi Angier, my beautiful wife Oriah for creating this awesome book cover and editing, and special thanks to Austin Scott for transcribing hours of these channeled messages for the making of this book. With love to my spiritual sons, my young Jedi's, Donte, Sharif and Elijah. Rock on!

Foreword

I got the nickname Riz The Wiz in 5th grade because I was the smart Indian kid who my classmates could cheat off of me on tests. I feel like they were the first to awaken me to being a wizard. I was born in Harlem, raised in the Bronx and my parents are from India. It was as crazy, strange, soulful, volatile and on edge, as you can imagine it to be.

I live in Southern Cali by the beach now with my wonderful wife Oriah, a shaman, author and fashion designer. It's my home. I never thought nor ever wanted to be a Trance Channel. I had my first psychic experience when I was 7 years old. I told no one. It never really stopped since then. As a kid, my dad sought my advice, in high school I was the one who everyone came to for guidance on their parents and their crushes and any other set of problems.

I always felt the answers that would help them and open their eyes more. When I sang in heavy metal bands and did musical theatre something would always "take over." Some other force of nature that was so precise and flowing and energized. A higher vibration. Looking back,

I see how this gift surfaced. I didn't know what was to come and how life would blast me into a very unexpected calling.

And for every gut-wrenching moment of agony I had from my mother, father and brother dying, I always felt some deep knowing of something bigger than all of us or something that was "One" with us. Call it the universe, or god or higher consciousness— I felt it and feel it more powerfully than ever before.

Thousands of people have seen my channeling all over the world since then. It is surreal. All I know is I sit down, I close my eyes, I let go...and the guides come through me and take over. They speak in unique accents and gestures, give insightful messages, answer questions and then I come back into my body...back from a strange sleep-like state. It's freaking magical and I'm in awe every time I do it. I'm here because I care about everyone being happier and more peaceful to themselves and to others.

Moments

Foreword by Oriah Mirza

Having been Riz's co-pilot and wife for ten years--supporting him, guiding him and being witness to the phenomena that lay before me--I always like to share my point of view of what my experience is like for those that are curious.

In our early years together I read the great channeled books of Seth Speaks by Jane Roberts and was fascinated by the role her husband Robert Butts shared—because I found myself in the same exact situation. Being witness to trance channeling of this caliber has always and will always be an astonishing event for me. After laying witness to 8,000 hours of recorded and transcribed full trance channeling sessions by Riz, and 2000 Circle of Light group gathering events in our home, yoga studios (home and abroad), and shamanic experiences; I have experienced more than the average person.

My enthusiasm and excitement for my husband's work has become my own expression as well, much like Robert Butts was always wanting to share his wife's work with the world. We consider ourselves Twin Flames, so it is fitting we share this book together. In this case, he decided to channel alone and recorded it on his iPhone and my assistant's fiancé, Austin transcribed it word for word. I did sit in on several of the chapters as they are channeled in final edit. I only edited the format and the punctuation and made the sentences a bit more suitable for reading. I passed it to our writer friend Julie, who also gave her punctuation and formatting input.

Each guide has their own inflections and their own individual cadences as they share their wisdom— it usually stems from their own personal experiences as a Personality Essence. When he channels a female energy, Riz's voice becomes softer and lighter, and when he channels a masculine voice it is noticeably more masculine and stronger, but it's still Riz's voice.

In the many weeks of editing, I became very familiar with the text, and one of the surprises that I encountered was when I was very still and quiet inside, I actually *heard* their voices in my head stating the sentence I was reading. The one that stood out to me was Diana. Maybe you can try this too, silent your mind while your reading and try to connect to them.

Some of the guides have a particular slang like Caravaggio; being an eccentric Italian Baroque painter, he tends to have noticeable linguistic nuances. I smoothed those words out after much deliberation, not wanting to remove his unique personality, but because I wanted the text to be absorbed as intended and I felt it would be a distraction.

Furthermore, the word 'god' was mentioned many times, and after extensive research I decided to not capitalize it — so you can determine what the definition of god is for you. I capitalized Oneness because I felt we all have the same definition of what Oneness refers to. I capitalized Source because also is commonly defined the same.

I created the book cover as well because, well, it's fun. This book will mark the beginning of many more channeled books in a series, including an angel book. I am fascinated and honored to help bring this book to your eyes and heart I am hoping you receive the same bountiful healing as I did.

Enjoy,

Oriah

Chapter 1 — 1st Key

The Key to Gratitude

November 2nd, 2019
Channeling 7:15 pm
Red Eagle Manor, Malibu, California

Riz Mirza

Here we go.
I'm just going to go into some meditation now, with no expectations; just an open blank page.

I have a vision of a roll of parchment paper and I unfurl it, and I feel the smooth, soft crinkles of the parchment.

And that begins to awaken, or still, my receiving; and even though there is background noise somewhere in the house, as my stepdaughter London is playing and laughing, I allow myself to understand that all sounds are blessed.

And I feel them get nearer the moment my heart turns to acceptance and love and surrender to all that is at this moment, without resisting or needing to control the environment.

For me, personally, it's just laying in a comfortable position with nice textures against my skin and a comfortable temperature, and that the lighting isn't harsh.

Breathe.

With each breath, different parts of my body relax. Sometimes a breath is—one that feels heavy as if I've been carrying something on my chest. Then I wonder if maybe it's just the presence of the guides that are coming through some—some field of energy, not a filter or a portal, but like water. It goes for everything. Because everything is one.

It's only the resistance to that fact that is the difference between peace and unrest.

Chief Red Eagle

Hello. I am Red Eagle. Gratitude is the ultimate painkiller. The power of gratitude disintegrates the most painful experiences of the past and the present—and even when your fear of the future frightens you, you can always rely on the power and the freedom and the connection that gratitude can bring to you.

Of course, it is easy to have gratitude when you are getting everything that you have wanted. And that can be a wonderful feeling to have gratitude flow in the joy that has come to you through your success; whether it is in love, or in your work—to create a life physically there must be some desire.

There must be some connection, then there must be conception, then gestation and nurturing. And then there are the rumblings of something about to happen soon— a birth. Can you have gratitude for the *process* of creation? It is certainly much easier to have this gratitude when a person is going to have a baby. You understand innately that it takes time for the baby's physical body to form, and you are in acceptance of this.

When you are creating other things in your life, it is harder to do so. You have very "defined" ideas of success. What is the key to success? Gratitude is the key to success. Through every step of your life path, within each moment, you have the opportunity to find magic.

Many only find the magic of a painful situation much later.

They call these moments realizing the lesson from the "bad-feeling" situation. The word "lessons" is not a very appealing idea. You do not want anyone to approach you and say "I am here to teach you a lesson." That would feel aggressive, and you would resist.

The key to finding gratitude is to not resist what is. The key to not resisting what is, is to have a very powerful core belief that everything is for *your evolution*—and for you to *choose* why you exist. If you choose that you exist because you wish to experience creation and discovery, and you realize that you are love itself, then this core belief will be firmly rooted in the Universe of You. It will permeate all the galaxies within your spirit: all the dimensions of your essence.

It will expand through your physical being with a peaceful, radiant, focused energy that is also fluid, spontaneous, and precise. No longer will you choose anger or sadness to center yourself. When you are in a tight spot, that is what people do, they either react in anger and lash out at something they do not like, or they sink into sadness, repeating the same bad feelings over and over again.

New and powerful core beliefs will change your life experience so powerfully that you will swear that everything has changed and people have changed how they behave or speak around you. But it will be the way you see everything that will have changed.

This is freedom. This is Self-Mastery.

The key to success is self-mastery. How do you define self-mastery?

Is it defined by a particular ability that you have—a skill that you have mastered? That would be mastering a *task* but not mastery of the *self*. What is the Self? First, let's define this.

The Self is you and you are a multi-dimensional being. What does that mean? What would you like it to mean? Do you like to be one-dimensional or multi-dimensional? If you know a person or a story that is **one** dimensional, then you can know what is **multi-dimensional**.

If a movie is one-dimensional, you will know it—it will feel flat. It will not have raw, unpredictable energy; a vibrating, pulsating, spontaneous energy with lots of hidden magic expressing itself in ways you did not expect; layers and layers of more complex and interesting qualities.

Endless, infinite.
This is you.

Look into a baby's eyes—you will see the universe shining in there. You were that baby too. That light is still within you, in fact, that light *is* you. Close your eyes for a moment—can you take a few moments now, as you read this, to check in with yourself and observe your body language right now? Are there any tense muscles in your face, your hands; your back, your neck?

Are you sitting comfortably? Are you distracted by noise or anything else in your physical environment?
Are you trying to focus very hard? Is your brow furrowed? Is your jaw tight? Are you breathing? How do you tell if something is alive? You check to see if it is breathing.

The most natural thing for a human being to do is to breathe; and yet, they do not teach you how to breathe more powerfully and effectively, to help your emotional moods: and how to draw in more energy into the physical body from the air.

The breath carries life force. You breathe life into yourself, into others, into your projects, into your home. Into your work. Into all creation. This is possible when you have surrendered to peace within you. It will show up in everything you do without any strain on your part.
And then the creation of that newness you feel from shifting your emotional energy begins to breathe life back into you—look what happens when you see a beautiful creation; when you hear it, when you taste it—it brings you life.

A great chef pours their magic into their food and when you eat it you feel that magic and your mood shifts and now you smile and pass the magic forward. As you are breathing life into things, you are also having things breathe life into you.

When you resist, you are not breathing. Breathing consciously and deeply is a practice. You must be reminded to breathe. For many of you who smoke, that is the only time that you are taking a focused deep breath. Most of the relief you feel is not coming from the thing you are smoking, but because you are breathing deeply when you inhale. It is the beautiful built-in self-healing mechanism of your body.

So breathe now, and let go a little bit more. This is the practice of surrendering to the present moment. When you are not surrendering to the present moment, you are living in the past or the future. You may feel that whatever is happening in the present is bad; then you will certainly need to breathe more than ever. Having more breathe and stillness is having more peace.

Maybe you don't trust stillness — maybe because you only feel alive when you are doing something. Perhaps silence is deafening and stillness is crippling to you. This will lead to an exhausting life, and you will grow more and more tired. You see, it takes a lot of energy to resist.
You must hold a lot of tension to keep a wall up; to keep a fortress up around you.

It is like a government that has a very high military budget. That budget is one of money, which also represents energy. But you spend a lot of energy on your defenses and your resistance. The whole notion of a fort is that you want to be ready for an attack.

The immune system of the body is a network of signals to keep it healthy. You may feel it is to protect you from disease, but then the focus becomes on protection from disease rather than the powerful, good, flowing feeling of being healthy. You see, when you change the way you talk about everything, you become more tuned to the magic of all experiences, because now you are operating from the new core belief that everything is part of your path and your path is one of creation, discovery, love, and peace. Look at these two words: reaction, and creation. They are the same letters. With one small change, the word has new meaning.

If you stay only in the reaction, you are now in an endless loop going over and over and over it again through the same feeling. When you take out the immediate reaction and see the magic of the situation, then you can create from it. When you are not creating, you are dead. When you are not breathing, you are dead. Figuratively and physically.

The life that you desire is defined by the amount of love you allow yourself to feel at any time—because you are love, it is natural to desire this. There will be some people who sit at a funeral and cry, and maybe there will be someone who is at a funeral who wants to laugh. It is socially acceptable to cry very strongly at a funeral, but it is not socially acceptable to laugh at a funeral. Generally, if you do laugh strongly at a funeral, they will consider you crazy, and ask you to leave—but not if you cry and roll on the floor and scream. That is not crazy, to most people. People understand pain more than joy.

Grieving is a natural process, *staying* in grief is not. If a person—in their core—feels love and joy, then they would know that the person who has passed away has gone on to a higher place, a higher dimension, an ascended state of being. They will grieve less, but the belief would have to be very powerful.

What if you wanted to laugh at the funeral of a friend? What if all you could do was think of the funny times you had together? What if the spirit of your friend was talking to you in your soul? "Look at my body there! I'm not dead, I'm *right here* with you!" Some people will think you are crazy for that.

Don't you believe in the eternalness of the soul? Do you believe that you continue afterward? What belief feels better to you? Since you cannot prove that you don't go on, and you cannot prove that you do go on, it all depends on what you are willing to believe; for some people, all the proof in the world is not enough for them to believe.

There are gifted mediums all over the world who have said things that they never could have known to their clients. They receive personal information during a reading, and the person feels great healing from that reading. The healing comes because, for them, this is proof that death was only physical, and the loved ones are still with them.

There is far more to reality than just what you know so far. You are *living proof* of the mystery. How did you get here? What belief is the "right" one? Maybe nobody can prove to you there is a god, and maybe nobody can convince you that there is no god, because the nature of your beliefs is your personal choice. I hope that you choose powerful beliefs for yourself. But wait a moment —what does powerful mean?

What is the nature of this word, "powerful?"

There have been people who are very "powerful" and did very terrible things to humanity. Their hate was powerful.

When we say, "have a powerful belief," it means that that belief can bring you the power of peace in all situations. No matter what you go through, that belief brings you peace.

Is there a higher vibration than peace? Yes. The highest vibration is celebration. Wouldn't you love to know every person on Earth after they are at peace, are now in celebration? Imagine the whole planet dancing, singing, smiling, in appreciation of life; celebrating eternally. That is the music of the Universe.

Nature does this; every stem, every flower, every tree is in celebration. It moves through the seasons with grace, rooted, receiving the light and opening up into the environment and going through the cycles: dries out, goes back into the Earth, comes up again.

When you find the Key to Gratitude, you will unlock yourself. When you use the Key of Gratitude, you open up the magic of the present moment. The present moment is now. And now...and...now. And NOW. The present moment is eternal. It is all you shall ever truly have—to *choose* peace.

Breathe deeply into your being now.

You can have a different experience reading this book more than any other book, and you can bring this experience to other books that you will read in your life too. Make a change now, and slow down.

Breathe light into your spine, relax every muscle in your face. Just try it. Relax your jaw. Relax your forehead, your eyebrows. Your eye sockets, your ears, your teeth, your tongue. As you read this you can do it. It will happen automatically. Relax your scalp, your shoulders. Relax your expression, and breathe again.

When a person comes out of a coma, it is a type of gratitude, unlike anything you've ever seen. Imagine a person in a coma for several months, in-between worlds as the body is working to reset. When you come out of a coma, your preferences, your pickiness, relaxes. When you come out of a coma, any place for lunch is good—isn't it? When you come out of a coma, all the faces you see are beautiful. When you awaken from that unconsciousness, the colors are rich, the shapes are interesting.

When you emerge from that darkness, you begin to see everything is alive and special. Maybe you have been in a coma for a long time, trying to reset, using all of your energy — trying to reset, at the same time — fighting battles, patterns; going over your past trauma relentlessly. You want to come out of a coma, don't you? I know the way out of this hell. Find gratitude. Gratitude is the key to coming out of a spiritual coma.

That is your rebirth! That is your Great Awakening.
Awakening to the beauty and the magic of living as You. The gift of getting to be you will finally make sense. Maybe in the past, you have had every reason and evidence to show you have not had a good life. Maybe your evidence is very compelling, and nobody would argue with you, that you have every reason to feel that life has not been good. You have proof.

We are not here to argue with you. We're here to speak to you about self-mastery. And if you don't want to be a slave anymore to the pain, then discover the peaceful power of Gratitude and it will bring you freedom from agony, the inner peace to not hate, to not live in anger at the past or the present, or even the future. Gratitude makes you timeless, and all of your creations will be timeless and authentic. You will have actual fulfillment simply from creating with this freedom in your spirit.

Your success will not be dependent on others' opinions of it. The success will be for you to know internal peace.

Clench your fists very tightly now, as tight as you can clench them. Breathe in and breathe out and open your hands. Let them go limp.

You cannot receive with a closed fist. A closed fist does two things: either it is gripping very tightly to something, a person or an idea, or a thing that they want to control, or it is ready to strike something, and cause some damage.
An open hand—shakes the hand of another person, pats another person on the back— an open hand is able to receive.

Do you feel resistance while trying to receive love? Maybe you just allow love in your life, but do you receive it? What is the difference? If you *allow* somebody to hug you, that is very different than *receiving* the hug in your being. The receiving is where all the feeling is. Receiving is up to you. How much you receive does not depend on how much someone gives.

You have the power to feel something big from something small. Use your sensitivity. This is what we mean by "surrendering to the embrace of life." Your internal reality is so powerful, that you can actually resist energy trying to get in. If a person tries to hug you and puts their arms around you, and you are mad at that person, you will not receive the love that they are trying to give you. You are gripping tight to whatever made you mad at them.

Perhaps they need to reassure you, or apologize, or say many sweet things to soften you and your resistance. And at some point, if they continue, you may let go. And you start to feel the love of the hug, and you breathe with the person you are receiving. This is "surrendering to the embrace of life." It is such a tender protected place within you, you may not want to think about it right now—you may just want to push this away because you have been so traumatized by what you have experienced.

Maybe you have only had a few great moments in your life, but in those moments what were the qualities that you experienced? If you examine the greatest moments of your life, you felt fully like yourself, "in the moment," that joy, the radiance of seeing yourself as whom you know yourself to be, or what you know yourself to be, which is love and magic.

In the greatest moments of your life, you were in awe of what was happening. In these moments you were fully present, awake to the experience, so present to the goodness, that it was almost like it was a dream.
Perhaps the greatest song of your world is the children's nursery rhyme:

"Row row row your boat
Gently down the stream
Merrily, merrily merrily, merrily
Life is but a dream."

To "row your boat gently" means you are absorbing every movement on the water. You are sensitive to the experience.

When you dream tonight, you will believe what is happening is real. There are many times you have woken up from a dream in the middle of the night, thanking god it was only a dream because it was terrifying, and other times wishing to god that it was still going on because the dream was so pleasant. You lay in your bed in this belief. "How could that have been just a dream? It was so real." All of you have said this to yourselves—not only once, but countless times throughout all the years you have been alive.

You had dreams like this when you were a child, a teenager; and now you have these dreams, and tonight, after you read this, you will again go into that world of the Dreamscape.

So all of those things that happen in the dream: feelings of pleasure, physical sensations, emotional states where you cry, so powerfully real—why do you call that a dream, and yet *this* is "reality?" What is the difference between this here now, as you are reading this book, and tonight when you are in the dream? What makes this more real than the dream?

You may say, "Because every day this is the same thing— I have the same house, I have the same body, it is more consistent. In the Dreamtime, the dream can change throughout the night. It can change even within the same dream; everything can change."

Your only proof to yourself, by your own admission, about whether the dreams are real or this life is real, is that this life, right now, is more consistent in the environment and people you know in it and lasts longer—a lifetime. It seems to keep going on, the dreams are just for a few moments, perhaps, but this thing you call "your life," it is the same and keeps going. So the only difference is the duration of time and consistency.

That is not a very good criterion for distinguishing between what is real and what is not real. When you die, what will this life be? Perhaps like a dream? It depends on your belief system. Let us say you believe that you go on, then you will be in a totally different environment when you leave this body, and everything will change in the environment; then this entire life will seem like a dream to you. That is why that nursery rhyme so powerful.

So what is the point or the answer to this exploration?
Firstly, there does not need to be a point in exploration, exploration is the point. Seeing something new is the point. Secondly, reality is defined by how you feel—not your physical environment. You may be at a party, where everyone is happy, and it is for a birthday celebration—maybe even your own birthday—but that does not decide whether you will be happy there. They all can be singing and dancing and smiling and laughing and you could be miserable inside. That would be your reality. Someone would say no—the reality is, you are in a room full of people who love you and are celebrating you. But there is

also another reality; *personal reality* and *that* is what defines your life.

Here is where you would have to practice how to receive so that you are not in your private, isolated world of protection. Have you noticed in your private, isolated world of protection, there is tons of pain? Looks like your protection is not so strong, eh? So now what will you do? Strengthen your defenses? Build thicker walls? Have more guard towers? Have more barbed-wire fences? More traps for the "enemy?"

Only the deserving will be able to come through all these defenses and get to you? Alright, let us say that they do get through all the defenses and get to you—they go through all the barbed-wire, get past all the armed guards, jump over the moat, tunnel through the land, climb the walls—and they reach you.

What are they going to get for all this trouble? Are they going to meet a peaceful, happy, joyous person, full of love? Is that who you think lives behind fortresses? They will come to realize they are dealing with a hostage-taker. Do you know what is a hostage situation? You might have heard, "You are holding yourself hostage." But, what does that *mean*?

The version of yourself that was what you considered to be "innocent, pure, magical"—the greatest version of yourself that you are protecting...maybe at some point in your life, maybe it was when you were a child—you began to protect this version of yourself. The version of yourself that could not understand why you were not seen and heard for the love that you are.

Why were these people around you so messed up? They did things to you. They did not do things for you. Whatever it may have been, with all the confusing messages they gave to you—you began to protect this version of yourself and lock them away until it was safe for them to come out.

So you have been working your whole life; creating, and building, and trying, and struggling, and striving, to create a life where somehow, that person can come out again—for it will be safe for them to finally come out— the magical one.

If the magical one is still locked up, then who are we talking to right now? The prison guard? We are talking to the hostage-taker. The hostage-taker has a list of demands —they always do, "Give me this, this, and this, and then I will release the hostage."

So you have a list of demands from the Universe. You have a checklist from your life. These are the things you **want**, and if you don't get it, *that's it*—you will not be happy. Whatever you have to do, you will do to get these things—or maybe not, maybe you will not even do what you will have to do to get these things, you have given up and become resigned.

But, you've just got that list, and that list has to be checked off; the list of demands.

You call them requests, you call them dreams, but inside, the essence is the same: if you don't get it, you're not happy. The is the hostage negotiations.

What happens if you don't give the hostage-taker some of those demands? They start to shoot some of the hostages, don't they? Yes, you begin to kill off parts of yourself. You let parts of yourself self-destruct because you don't get what you want the way that you want it, and when you want it. So you will suffer and start to die inside.

What else does the hostage-taker want after the demands are met? They want their safe passage to freedom once they get what they want. Hey, don't consider them a criminal, just let them escape to another country afterwards. You know, it is the old classic story of hostage-takers; they always want to go live somewhere else afterwards "peacefully" but, only after they have gotten everything they wanted violently and forcefully.

Perhaps we are in a hostage-taker situation, and we have to negotiate with you. We are in a hostage negotiation situation. So, why are you doing this to yourself? Aren't you tired of hurting yourself? We will ask you this one more time. Take a breath. Get sober *right* now, do not get intoxicated or distracted by thoughts.

Maybe these words are coming from your future self, in this book, staring back at you—you don't *know*. Your future self that is already free, and surrendered to the magic that they are fully. So we ask you again, are you tired of hurting yourself?

If you are truthful, this is where you will begin your rebirth. This is where you will find everything you have ever wanted. The Key to Gratitude is to not hurt yourself anymore. The Key to Not Hurting Yourself Anymore is Gratitude.

You will come to know gratitude is such a new powerful way of being, that you will even have gratitude for gratitude. It is that massive of a gift. And you will no longer be a hostage or a hostage-taker. You will no longer be in a coma. You will no longer be isolated. You will no longer be in the past or the future. You will be out here with all of us—having fun. You will do this so powerfully that you will realize that actually there is no "inside or outside". There never was, there is only Oneness. The Key to Gratitude and the Gift of Gratitude is *surrendering* to Oneness and Feeling Free.

Bless you.

Chapter 2 — 2nd Key

The Key to Peace

November 4th, 2019
Channeling 4:40 pm
Red Eagle Manor, Malibu, California

Riz Mirza

So...here we are. I always begin by closing my eyes and taking a deep breath. I try to inhale through my nose, but sometimes I feel not enough big air comes through, so I have to breathe through my mouth deeply. And as I feel the air, and I follow its path into my body, I see where it goes. I see my stomach rise and I try to imagine a path opening into my heart.

I begin by closing my eyes and relaxing my face. I like to be laying down with my buckwheat pillow under my neck; it's my favorite pillow because it adjusts to where my neck is most comfortable in that moment. I can hear sounds in the house. I can hear my assistant Erika preparing the room for the channeling later this evening. I hear muffled laughter of my wife, Oriah speaking to someone, somewhere in the house, and the sun is setting over the ocean and the Manor is taking a long breath with me. It feels—I feel.

I visualize that I surround myself with a big fuzzy warm light and I start to let my body go. I let the bed support me, and feel it's strength...I let the Earth support me. I feel myself leaving. The only way that I can describe this feeling is that I become very still and very open and my body drops away. I don't know what to expect, I just trust —I don't know who will come to channel this next chapter, even at this moment while I am speaking this. All I know is there is love and I am surrounded in it. I am now feeling a presence.

I suspect it is Guinevere.

She is a Spirit Guide who has come in many forms to different people over time, but most know her, or think of her, as a mythological character or literary character in the story of King Arthur as his wife the Queen. She is an actual Spirit Guide who made her presence known by coming into people's minds and imagination—the so-called imagination—and channeled her messages over time.

The author, creator or receiver of her messages receive her wisom and transmutes her eternal love into many forms that we enjoy today. That is my best explanation of her, she is not a myth, she lives. I have felt her with me for years as one of my guides.

She usually in the past, only shows up for me in times of great personal pain, and thankfully today, she is coming to me to only dictate this chapter. She comes to me now when I am at peace in this new way, and I feel she has come to speak about peace. She's here.

Guinevere

Some believe that peace is fragile, that at any moment, something may happen to disturb the peace. A fire may be lit that creates destruction or chaos. Nerves are raw and some believe that just under the surface of peace, war is dormant. You can feel this energy in certain people that you meet. There is a beautiful smile or pretty words that come from them.

They say nothing wrong, and yet, perhaps you sense something is amiss—that under their calm exterior, there is a storm. Is war necessary to find peace? Is it really the calm before the storm? Or is there a storm before the calm? As you quiet your mind, you will hear the whispers of the ancients. The Ancients are also timeless. They are ancient to you, yet they are beyond time and when you refer to them as Ancients, it is because you are also recognizing that you yourself are eternal.

With every graceful beat of your blessed heart, with every firm and gentle step you take upon this Earth, with every breath that you breathe, may you feel peace. Is peace the opposite of war? No, celebration is the opposite of war. After many battles, after wars have been won, the victors celebrate. The planet will achieve an era that will be eternal where there are no more physical wars.

This will be, of course, achieved much more quickly when the peace is within. When one is imprisoned, shackled, isolated, punished, banished, alone, alone with other prisoners—how do they find peace? Peace amongst the chaos?

When loneliness haunts you, what do you do? Can loneliness bring forth messages?
Is the message that you, indeed, are unloved, or is loneliness haunting you repeatedly to bring you to a much more powerful realization? Some do not wish to go any further into finding peace, for they are tired. There is disappointment everywhere.

They do not trust those who offer teachings. They have become disillusioned with their heroes and it is as if they are sitting in a war council of some kind, wondering what to attack next; the ego—which they have just learned to despise; the mind—which they do not trust; the heart— which is quivering with fear and trauma; or the intellect —which they worry has become a set of programs and false information.

When you are utterly physically exhausted, you must surrender to laying on the ground and letting the body breathe as it must during great exhaustion. Panting. Gasping for more life-giving breath. The same is true for the heart, the mind, the intellect—you must rest. But exhausting yourself so far has been the only way to surrender. Rest in peace. Why is this said only in reference to death? You wish for your loved ones to rest in peace. Is life all about battling internal wars where only death shall bring rest and peace?

May you rest in peace throughout your existence, throughout your lifetimes, throughout your day, throughout your night, through all of your existences in every dimension.

You are not your gender, your ethnicity, your economic background, your religion, your name, even. You have chosen this human form in this lifetime to move through war into peace and into a joyful celebration. Do not get too used to the form you are in. As you look in the mirror, whether it is pleasant to you or unpleasant to you, what you see reflected back at you—you are only this form for a time.

Have you forgotten the music of your soul? The music of your soul is the resonance of all the beautiful systems of magic and love unique to your vibration as a living being, extension, and source of everything. You wish to find peace through balance. You believe a balanced life is a harmony between your practical life and your spirituality. You wish to find a balance and integrate them better. There is a way to balance the practical and the spiritual. You will be free of that exhaustion when you realize there is no difference between the two.

Everything is "spiritual." All of reality is in perfect unfolding in complete alignment with creation. You may find this difficult to accept for perhaps you wish for a world free of pain. You must free yourself to free others. There is no separate spiritual path from the so-called material path. You can find Spirit in anything and everything. You will find Spirit in birth and Spirit in death.

You decide how to receive it and understand it. Your personal victory will be in your surrender to understanding this; that your *entire existence* is your spiritual path. You cannot run from it, you cannot step away from it; **wherever you step shall be your spiritual path.**

Whether you destroy yourself by being at war with yourself or struggle for peace with yourself and your surroundings; whether you do this for a year or lifetimes, whether you isolate or embrace all that is; your spiritual path will be everything you experience. Every move you make or do not make, every thought you think or do not think, every addiction that you heal or do not heal, all of it is your spiritual path. Your surrender to this along with a very good sense of humor shall bring you more and more peace.

Burning deep down inside you there is a light. It cannot be extinguished. You may cover it with layers of pain. You may deprive it of air, sustenance, to no avail— it will not go out, for it is *not sourced* by your emotions and your reactions to the unfolding of your life. This light is *what you are*. It shall remain, whether you choose to live or you choose to die. Do not take your own life by your hands; there is no honor in this, nor shall you find solace. You will still be on the Path and have to learn in this lifetime or after.

Do you know what honor can be?

You honor the process of creation and healing when you choose to redefine everything for yourself; god, love, peace, fun, boredom. All of them are up to you — defined by you and if you let that light within you choose for you, then you shall create and discover the most powerful definitions beyond what you have ever realized before.
Redefining these things to suit your life to be free of conflict; free of enemies, knowing that all of it is to teach you — that is redefinition.

Teach yourself to be your truest self. When you surrender to your truest self, you will discover that the Key of Peace is in your pocket It has always been in a beautiful pendant around your neck, covered by layers of clothing to protect your heart. There are no mountains that are bigger than you. The cosmos is not bigger than you.

When you see all of these things, they are reflected in your eyes; they can all fit inside the reflection in your eyes. What if you were to take this in? What if you were to believe in this? What if you cease to be so hard on yourself and others? This is part of the Key of Peace.

You are safe in your life.
You are safe in your death.
You are safe in the beating of your heart.
You are safe in each and every blessed breath.
You are safe to shed tears.
You are safe to release fears.
You are safe under a darkened sky.
You are safe to fall or fly.

You are safe to know more than you know.

You are safe to stay or to go.

You are safe to open the doors that appear.

You are safe to sit or to stand and cheer.

You are safe to share a bit of your love.

You are surrounded by god, not just from above.

You are one with the Divine.

You are safe to remember.

You are safe to realize the victory is found in your surrender.

You are safe in your skin.

You are safe to begin.

You are safe to be blessed.

You are safe when it's all a mess.

You are safe from the rain—you are safe in the rain.

You are safe to gaze with love at the origins of your pain.

You are safe to tell your stories, and you are safe to hear theirs too.

You are safe to know togetherness is the safety you can choose.

Is there someone you have not made peace with? It is possible to have peace with that person even if they are no longer living, even if you cannot find them, or even if they refuse to speak with you? To carry the sound and fury of war within you, not only destroys you bit-by-bit, but you reduce your positive impact on those around you and in all your creations. You cannot carry or create masterpieces with your paintbrush if you are at war yourself or another.

The Key to Peace is knowing it is up to you. To declare peace comes from the *surrender* to peace, but you cannot do this by *pretending* to be peaceful.

Just to have a peaceful face and smile, or to say peaceful, pretty words that you have learned, that only thickens the war-soup within you.

To not react does not mean that you are peaceful. First, you must surrender to a new belief, and perhaps it will be a challenge for you—perhaps you will feel there are exceptions to this belief, but I can assure you, you will not find peace if there are exceptions. You must believe and know that everything was divinely created by you and for you.

All of it, every experience, was created by your Higher Self. That Higher Self is also the light that is within you that cannot be destroyed. It is the eternal you, throughout any lifetime regardless of gender, ethnicity or status. All your past lives are You. You are not separate from it. Your awareness is expanding to be able to realize yourself—to be able to realize that you are the light, and you have gone into a pattern of fear and inner wars.

This is why you are a human being in this stage of your existence, you are gifted with self-reflection. The animals on the planet are not here for self-reflection; they are here to be your teachers, your guides, and your playmates, and your helpers. Animals are fully who they are at all times; they are fully expressed.

Their purpose here is not for self-reflection or expansion — yours is. You may consider this new belief system that I offer you, we may have a peaceful agreement between us that we sign on the parchment of eternity. Imagine the parchment unfolding, and in your hand is an exquisite pen. And we sign an agreement in this declaration of inner peace that every bit of your experience was divinely orchestrated by you — in co-creation with all — all people, all things, all environments, all experiences.

This declaration carries and resonates an energy, that will release the past, the present and the future from resistance and pain. As you practice and surrender to this belief, you will slowly and powerfully begin to see the tiniest bits of magic revealing itself in every moment to you. Peace is an active vibration. It is not dead. *It is not a boring feeling.*

It is an endless opening that you feel throughout every bit of your being, and you can experience this without moving a muscle — without even having a conversation with someone you are at war with. When you declare peace within yourself, there shall be peace; and either instantaneously or eventually, the other person shall feel it too.

When you choose peace this way, then you are able to make decisions to take care of your physical bodies, your properties, and possessions and loved ones more powerfully. If you have been in physical danger, then by declaring peace within yourself, you shall create a new environment. You shall not be afraid to leave it behind you; your declaration of peace shall carry you, shall burn bright in that core of what you are: that light to a new life. You will leave the violence behind you.

You will bow your head to the majesty of peace. You will breathe in peace, you will breathe out peace. You are the Key of Peace, and peace is the key to your freedom.

Bless you.

Live in peace. Rest in your life peacefully. You shall hear the wonderful music coming through the walls of your resistance and encompassing your soul to surrender in victory and dance in your spirit in the celebration of everything.

The Key to Peace: Part II

Chapter 3—continuation.

King Arthur

I am Arthur, and I greet you in peace. I greet you from my state of being, which is peace.

The words I speak come from peace. The vibration is the undercurrent of every communication from me to you.
Must there be war to achieve peace? What occurs in a war? Death, and confrontation. Pain. A desperation for survival. Meeting one's self on the battlefield, for that is what one soldier—that is what one knight faces in the other who is fighting for the same reasons, to defend their kingdom, their home.

Fortresses are created to defend and protect a kingdom. Walls are erected, traps are set, and guards are stationed at the watchtowers. An arsenal and an army are always at the ready. Perhaps you feel it is the nature of life, in its uncertainty you are certain that others will try to take or destroy that which you have built. With this belief comes the evidence you have gathered. But if you are wise, then you will consider re-examining the evidence for deeper meaning and if you are seeking deeper meaning, then this means you are seeking freedom and peace of mind.

For some, the battle is an inner battle. For some, the tyrant—the dictator—lives inside, and rules with an iron hand, telling you you are not doing enough, you do not have enough, and you yourself at your very core are not enough.

Lack leads to wars. Empires are created by invading, and it is often called expansion. I am not here to debate what seems to be a part of the history of peoples. There are tribes all over the world, throughout every era that you know of as it is recorded, and these tribes have engaged in battles and sought the expansion of their territory, their culture, and their legacies.

On the other side of this force will be the one that feels invaded, brutalized and attacked. The side that feels they did nothing wrong, and nothing to deserve this aggression. Many will argue that there were many benefits of this constant battling between peoples, that great civilizations were produced by this dynamic interaction.

The fight, the victory, the defeat, the claiming of properties and peoples, the establishing of a new order; and so it goes throughout the history of the physical world. But I am here to speak to you of the metaphysical world. The world of your understanding. The universe of your mind. To find the Keys to Peace, to be victorious in this battle, you must surrender.

The Key is the surrender of your inner war. Do you know what you are surrendering to? Many things. You must consider surrendering to the magic that is inherent in all experiences, be it pleasurable or painful. You must expand powerfully your perspectives and understandings beyond the conceptual. It means that you must realize this in your spirit. For if a thing has spirit, you are affected by it. You are moved by its power; you are awakened by its light as if you were asleep.

If you wish to be a king or a queen, then understand this: a bad king rules the people and serves himself, but a good king serves the people and rules himself. What does it mean to serve? Could service be a Key to Peace?
Service must be done from love, or it will not carry the vibration of healing. Love for what? Love for existence, which will require gratitude. Gratitude is certainly the key —one of the Keys to Peace.

To have love for your existence means that you are accepting that you are eternal. Your existence is more than your lifetime. You have lived many lifetimes. Your existence is forever.

If there is no feeling of love, you will not get very far in service to the world or ruling yourself. What does it mean to rule yourself? You are referring to self-mastery. Self-mastery is not the skill that you are able to perform very well—whether it is chopping wood or preparing food.

Self-mastery is the ability to shift from a bad feeling emotional place to a better one without needing anything at all to change, be it a person or a situation or an outcome. If you are able to do this without moving a muscle from where you are, without needing to change your physical environment, without needing to hear words from someone else, without needing to hear good news, then you are experiencing self-mastery. This is a great leap for anyone to take, but it is a worthwhile leap.

You must give yourself this gift. It will help you be free of the wars that you have been fighting for so long. Your shield is heavy and your sword exhausted and hammered from giving and receiving blows, from blocking attacks, and your helmet prevents you from breathing the fresh air.

Your iron boots are making you feel heavier than you are. It is time to remove the suit of armor. It is time to drop the shield and the sword and to remove your helmet. It is time to breathe the fresh air, to not be afraid to feel what you have been longing to feel throughout so many eras of your life.

You are not numb, though you may think you are. You still *feel* underneath your numbness.

You have just frozen, become stoic, unable and unwilling to let them know that you are shaken. There have been moments where you wish you could have disappeared. You wish you could have let it all go, to leave this place forever.

To be done with it. Too much fighting. Too much lack of sympathy and empathy. Too much selfishness and cruelty. You do not understand how it can be so chaotic and dangerous in this world. That the evil ones are in power. The soulless ones who rule, perhaps you are convinced of this and cannot be unconvinced. Perhaps you feel to declare peace within yourself and to choose love and joy is no longer an option, for it is unrealistic to you.

Perhaps you feel you must defeat those forces and you will dedicate your life to this cause, whether it is with your words, your anger, or your actions. Who knows when you will be satisfied, if ever? Some of you have declared for yourself that you will die trying in your attempts for peace in the world. That is if enough people die then there shall be peace. Perhaps it will be when there are none left or perhaps when only one small group who has emerged victorious over all the battles shall rule the Earth. Is it that you believe?

Perhaps you feel you cannot be happy or joyful or peaceful as long as there is evil and mayhem, as you see it. Whatever it is that you declare — it shall be. Perhaps you feel that to be at peace with something means that you cannot change it and have accepted defeat. This could not be further from the truth, and this is where the Sword of Truth must be wielded powerfully.

The Sword of Truth is to cut through illusion. What is an illusion? Is it an illusion if you were to see the great Oak tree breathing, its bark ebbing and flowing with vibration? Would it be an illusion to see the energetic life force aura around another person? Or is it an illusion when you do not see these things—when you regard them as inanimate or simply "alive" in the scientific sense?

Are the pages of this book alive, physically? If you were to place these pages under a powerful instrument that could see into its atoms and molecules, would you see pulsating, radiating atomic structures? Indeed, you would. And so, not only are the pages alive in the physical perception, according to the instruments that you use. They are also alive with the potency and the energy of the words you are reading and receiving. Some, you are allowing this book into your system of belief, and some of you are doing your best to hold back.

Holding back to observe, to ponder, to filter through your database of beliefs, to see if it is worthy of your acceptance. If the words are wise enough to penetrate your fortresses and to get past your guard tower. What is this treasure you are guarding behind these walls?

What is behind your walls? What is this great treasure within you that you are protecting? Is this treasure powerful? Does it contain abundance and great energy? How is it serving you? And who is that person who is protecting this inner magic, this inner wealth?

If indeed, this power is as vibrant as you claim it is, so much so that you have created an empire around you to protect it, then how is its power being used? Why does it even need protection unless it is only living for itself and not interested in serving others? Or is it only serving others through prison bars? Yes, perhaps you have been living in such a way that the bars of the prison are invisible. You have been shaking hands with people through the bars of the prison. You have been eating your meals through the bars of your cell. Perhaps you are even embracing others, hugging them, but between you still, there are these barriers.

You know they are there, and others, perhaps, know they are there; and others cannot quite put their finger on it, but they cannot become intimate with you. This is not the prison of the mind, for the mind is neutral; it is not evil. These are the prisons of your reactions, which are based upon the beliefs that you hold. When you believe that something should be one way and it is not that way, then you declare it to be bad. When something matches what you would like it to be, then you declare it to be good.

And so, your life becomes this repetitive, narrow experience. You are not a master if this is how you are living. You are a slave. Enslaved to always trying to feel better, and never able to maintain the feeling, even if you achieve it. Is peace actually peace, if it is fragile? You will then say, "my peace is so strong, no one can shake it." Again, you are believing that there are forces trying to shake it.

This would then mean that you do not believe that everything is for your benefit, for your evolution, for your freedom, and ultimately, your peace. So you resist those forces because you believe that they are in opposition to your peace. But the one who has mastered themselves sees *every situation* as the opportunity for greater peace, for when you expand your understanding of all situations — when you begin to see and believe that there is great magic of transformation in all situations, then you will see a much wider and greater peace.

It is not peaceful strength when you feel you have to defend it. Peace allows all things to be felt without sinking into some feeling of destruction or chaos. It is fluid. It is permeable and adapts to all situations. One who is at peace is not at odds with their environment. They are at peace in public, and they are at peace in private. They are at peace in places they may not even want to be in, but they find their peace there.

To be more at peace, you must release all judgment. If you are judging others, you cannot be at peace. But you still believe there are "others". You will say, "I am one person and they are another." And yet you wish for Oneness on the planet. Logically, you believe that if all were to come together as One, there shall be peace. But where is Oneness within you? You believe, still—in opposition. There are those who support you, and then there are those who are your enemy to some degree and very quickly, you are back in the cycle of war.

What does it mean to be at war within yourself? Some will say, "I am at war with my mind. I can trust neither my heart nor my head. I am in my head," or "I am too much in my heart, and both have caused me great pain." And so, lack of trust is one of the reasons for war.

Or you do not trust that there will be enough resources. And so, one must feed off of another's resources, rather than to work interdependently. You see, there is no such thing as independence. There is not a living thing that is independent. The entire scope of the universe and all of reality is interdependent. Not even the tree is independent, or the mountain. The tree needs the sunshine and the rain, and the wind, and the soil, and throughout life, you shall find interdependence.

When you are in isolation, you are in denial of this interdependence. You must take a very deep breath here and now, and another. Let us continue.

When you open the doors of your kingdom, in peace, this means that you are happy to give freely, for you are abundant and your abundance is constantly being replenished. For you are surrendered to all of creation, and you do not hold any prejudices as to what is creation. You regard everything as creation.

For even destruction is part of creation; one may say that when the leaves fall from the trees, when they wither and die and fall to the ground, and the ground absorbs them, that they are destroyed; and yet, they are becoming part of the soil and re-absorbed. And new growth shall come in time, as the seasons are quite wise.

You refer to your state of being and the processes of your personality as your nature. You refer to the physical growth of plants on the planet as "nature," the "elements" of wind, sun, and water, and the stars, and the Earth, as "nature." You also have "elements." You are earthy, you are fiery, you are watery, or airy, or celestial. You are all of these. You are nature itself. Is nature at peace? There is lightning. There are tornadoes and tsunamis and fires and earthquakes and meteors striking the Earth. Is this peaceful?

These natural elements have taken the lives of people and animals, have created great marks upon the Earth that shall never change. There are great expanses of land that were discovered to be craters formed from objects from your outer space striking the Earth, and now they are great wonders of natural beauty. Is nature peaceful? Is peace quietude and stillness? If so, then only a garden would be peaceful. Perhaps you do not regard lightning as peaceful.

This will take a great leap of consciousness for you to realize that nature is peaceful. You will have to redefine peace if you declare nature to be peaceful, and the animal kingdom. They are attacking and eating one another with no remorse. All animals are in understanding of life and death. They are capable of love, for certainly they nurture their young. And yet, they shall also kill to protect them or to simply feed themselves. Or simply to protect their territory, or to prevent others from dominating them in any way. Is this peaceful?

Perhaps peace is the natural order of things. Perhaps you are at war with the natural order of things. Perhaps you believe that it is fine for the animal kingdom—unless of course, something has eaten your pet, then you are horrified.

What disturbs your peace? Simply put, anything that happens that you do not wish to happen, that you do not find to be pleasant or acceptable. And yet, all these elements of nature, you would probably agree, are part of the life force of Earth and necessary for the earth to remain vibrant, and to keep growing and rebirthing itself, as it does in every season. Then, perhaps the entire process is peaceful.

What about your nature? If you declared that your nature is peaceful, what would it mean to you about your life? It would mean—perhaps to you—that very little pain is felt; that you are prosperous and free from danger. Therefore, there is peace. If this is your definition, then much work would have to be done for this type of environment to be maintained at all times. And for many, a lifetime spent creating that is time well spent.

But what if you have never needed protection? What if your emotions have never needed protecting? Remember the treasure? Is not the treasure inside of you your magic? Is it not the Source of your existence—that cannot be taken from you—even by you? It is eternal, and that will be up to you to decide.

We are not here to convince you—but wish this for you as your friends. If you wish for peace, then you must declare it. If you are at war or estranged from a loved one, it shall be your decision to declare peace. This can be done whether your loved one is physically alive or has passed on to the next life. They need not be in your physical presence for you to declare peace with them. Peace can only come with understanding. What must you understand about them? Do not personalize this, understand this about reality; that each person is on their soul path of freedom and peace of mind.

When you understand the process, as you are seeing it for yourself in your own life, then you shall begin to have reverence for life itself and the journey of all. When you have reverence for the cycle of blame and victimhood, of fear and sadness, of desperation and greed, of loneliness, of violence—when you see that this comes from not surrendering to the love that you are—a very powerful new logic shall dawn on you and burst within you. And that is that we are all One. That the more you resist Oneness, the more wars, small and great, shall be suffered by you.

Perhaps this is a lifelong practice. So is bathing your body. It would be illogical to say, "Why must I bathe again when I have only bathed recently?" It would be immature to create a war about bathing or any other human need of the physical body. And so, peace must be practiced.

It is a worthwhile practice and a fulfilling one to do eternally. When you know that you shall surrender to peace eternally, you shall be less tired. The suits of armor shall disappear from your blessed body. You cannot feel anything in a suit of armor. If you were holding an infant in your arms while wearing a suit of armor, you will not be able to feel the infant, nor shall the infant be able to feel you. If you long for tenderness, then surrender to the tenderness of peace as a choice.

The peace that we speak of is not only the personal peace of your environment, your communications, and your actions; but a more expansive, cosmic perspective, and that is knowing that peace is an eternal process, for there are always deeper levels of peace.

Most have experienced inner wars that led to peace once the inner wars have been won. And so, that is what is occurring in the world as well. Somewhere, deep within the individual and the masses, and the so-called powers that be, wars are fought for control of resources and certainly — as of late — its energy.

Sources of fuel have become the cause of war. Nations fight for access to sources of energy — this fuels their great futility that permeates this ongoing aggression — that oil, the fuel source itself, is a limited source of fuel.

It is not sustainable, nor renewable, nor clean-burning; perhaps the nations shall deplete that resource, and then, and only then, will they turn to finding a resource that is unlimited.

Some wish for free energy technology to be revealed, and we are speaking to you about your own unlimited source of free energy that is within you. And that is, once you surrender to peace within you, you have access to this energy. This energy is love, this energy is magic. You have many activities that you do to reset you, to re-energize you; whether it is a pleasurable activity or a transformational activity that you learn such as yoga or meditation.

There are many ways that you have discovered to reactivate and replenish your energy. When you do not have this, then you feel drained. When you are drained, you isolate or become agitated and desperate for relief.

This is what nations do when they are fighting wars for resources. You, perhaps, begin to fight a war within yourself for resources.

This shall keep happening until you surrender to a source of energy that is limitless, and is self-renewing; that is, *your peace*. Your peace is not stagnant. It is not simply an acceptance of everything as it is, with no possibility of change. When you are at peace, then you are no longer "tripped up" by desperate or chaotic emotions. You are coming from and approaching *from* creativity, discovery, and awareness. You are surrendering to self-mastery. Peace is not emotionless, it is clean-burning, pure emotion that heals you, speaks through all of your creations, and is felt by others.

Some will not feel it, no matter what you do. Let it go. It is still about you, your reactions and understandings of the reality of your path. This includes everything and everyone. Make peace with that. When you are at peace, your body shall breathe perfectly. As you surrender to peace, the magic of life will be seen reflected in the new light of your new awareness.

Bless you.

Chapter 3 — 3rd Key
The Key to Creativity

November 7th, 2019
Channeling 7:15 pm
Red Eagle Manor, Malibu, California

Riz Mirza

Alright, I'm just relaxing my being—slowing all my systems down. Sometimes it takes a lot to shut down anything that is upsetting me or conversations that I don't wish to have during my day, sometimes right before I sit down to channel. And I know that this is part of my path also.

As much as I would like to control my environment, and have everything be extremely quiet, and have everything feel "peaceful" according to my standard of peace, I know that one of the most powerful things that a human being can do is find the Keys to Peace themselves.

I feel the next Guide integrating his being with me—as if I'm two voices speaking in harmony right now…in sync, every word. I feel the Spirit Guide in harmony with me, or maybe I'm in harmony with him. I don't know the melody is right now. I don't even know if this is me speaking right now or the Guide, this happens all the time. I think it's me, but as I surrender deeper, as I'm doing right now—by letting myself feel safe—I think that the message is already starting. And Caravaggio is here.

Michelangelo Merisi da Caravaggio

I am Caravaggio.

There are some painters who have a brush with only one hair on the brush. Can you imagine, to be so precise? To care so much as to put just one tiny line in the painting, so thin—just one hair?

They say god is in the details. Some people paint with broad strokes in life; you call them the simple people and the ones who are very complex, they are in their head. They are too picky, they are too hyper-focused. To paint with broad strokes is say, "I live for love, for my friends, the people, the beauty all around me," to laugh, to cry, to make love, and to be in love with creation—creation is the highest form of expression that people believe in.

That is why god is not called anything but The Creator. He is not called The Do-er or The Seer, he is called The Creator. She is called The Creator. And so that means that creation is what everybody holds in the highest regard. Your soul is moved by powerful creation.

From art to music, to architecture, to the dance, to the movie. And just a little bit of this changes your life, inspires your life forever. Just a moment in a movie, just the melody in a song, just the light effects in a painting coming down from the heavens, or the shine in the eyes —maybe the difference is just one stroke. Maybe made by the paintbrush with just one hair. And that tiny stroke gives a reflection of light in the painting that catches your eye. When the light is reflected in what you create, then the creation makes a difference. When you see that light reflected back to you in music, in dance, then the creative energy is transferred to you. Now, what are you going to do with it?

Sometimes the creative energy given to you by beautiful creations around you and it stays inside you for a long time and you do nothing with it. And sometimes, it just changes you; makes you happy, makes you want to tell somebody you love them because the creative force is everything. All of reality is the creative force. The power of the creation can make you sad, like a sad song. The vibration carried the light, the reflection of the feelings of the artist. And they land inside you and connect to you, and your pain, and your joy.

Do not take for granted all of the different types of creation just because you don't like some of them. This is not a good quality to have—that you only respect creations that you like. You have got to respect creation for creation's sake. Respect the process and what it takes to create something honestly, authentically with inspiration. Go beyond your preferences, your style, your choices. When you understand the nature of creation, you'll have reverence—that is a very good word to know — because reverence is not in your mind, reverence is in your soul.

Reverence is the energy that makes you bow to the energy that you see around you. Sometimes you can only get that in nature, but you get it when you see creation in a powerful way anywhere. It keeps you humble and grateful.

Negative opinions are just to entertain your mind for a little while. But ultimately, it does nothing for anybody. Give yourself the gift of recognizing the creative process of your life; not because you want to see it finished and perfect, but to know it can never be finished completely and it is always perfect because it is always growing. You do not look at your child and say, "You will be perfect when you are six; now, you are only three." Do you not see the beauty of being three? What about four? What about five?

And so, do not do this to yourselves or to others...you live in a competitive society. Who is the best? Who is the best filmmaker? So you give awards. That is just an opinion. What does it mean to be the best? It is a popularity contest by only a few people who are being asked. But if you ask the people, "Who is the best filmmaker?" You will get a very different answer than the people who get to vote for the movie. Everything will be a bit different if you ask the people what they feel is "the best."

You want to be the best, or you want to be your best? What does it mean to be the best? You want everybody to like you and to say you are the best? You give everyone this power. What if they say you are the worst? Then you become a slave to the opinions of others, and that is where you waste your precious, blessed energy, instead of creating from the magic of what you are, you begin to play the game to please everybody, and that is only because maybe you want to make money. Money is a beautiful thing, money is energy; do not make it wrong. But you must create from a place of freedom if you want to have a long life of creating.

What did you want to unlock in your creativity? What does it mean to be blocked in creativity? First, you've got to know what creativity is, because you create every day. We do not mean your schedule. You may create a plan; you create breakfast; you create a conversation. Maybe these kinds of creations bore you because they are routine and not spontaneous. You get very bored in the routine. When you are not creating you are dead. You feel frozen. You feel like you are slowly freezing—like the room is getting dark and you are tired. No inspiration.

But you want extraordinary creation. You want to make some things that you look at and know it is the best part of you. It is showing, expressing the true you. You have to go beyond the mind; the mind that is telling you that you cannot do it, it is not good enough, it is never going to happen—nobody's ever going to like it.

If you want to feel free, think about this, lots of people create something that is not true to who they are. But they like the money, so they keep doing it. There is nothing wrong with that if they are at peace with it; maybe they do something to make money, and make enough money for their liking, and they just want to live life to have fun and to spend the money they make.

They are not so committed to their creation, because to them their creation is actually money, and to others — it is how they are doing whatever they are doing that gives them the satisfaction. There is mastery in this. Being interested in how you do anything means you are present, aware and can create honestly with spontaneity. What inspires you to know you can have creation occur right now? Is it love or creation again?

You want to direct your energy into creation, and what blocks you? You cannot look away from this. You are at a point in the road to decide to reclaim your gifts for yourself. You have to want the feeling.

Why are you so mad? We've got to sit here and convince you to create? To not be mad about what you're creating? To tell you it is good? So many people can tell you what you create is good, but inside, you still don't think it is good. That is torture. If you want to help people, then you must do it with your heart — then show your work.

And wherever you're going to help, help. And you keep going because you keep growing, and you keep listening, and you keep transmitting you what learn from the Universe.

You learn to take the steps. You learn to break the patterns of laziness. Laziness has a lot to do with fear. Fear that it is not going to be good, fear that nobody's going to see you, fear that you're going to get rejected. That is where the laziness comes from. That is where boredom comes. You are bored because you don't see what is really going on. If you could see, deep into dimensions of where you are sitting right now, reading this book, you would see that you are the center of the Universe.

You are at the center of all dimensions of time and space; that is what your life is. You are a spirit that is eternal and you are focused on this reality right now. That is what your life is: focused reality created with your intention as a soul to learn about creation. But they don't tell you this in school. They don't tell you this in religion. It is not clear.

How are you going to dump all of this old stuff? The Key to Creation is to surrender. Surrender to the magic. Do not be so obsessed with the boredom and the disappointment, because boredom and disappointment can be so strong, the pain from rejection countless times in your life can be so strong, but you know that's not going to get you anyplace. You've just got to get up and show what you've got.

Don't be confused. When you get too confused, it is because you don't think you are safe. If you make this choice, or you make that choice, you think your safety comes from whether it's going to work out for you in the way that you want it. "Should I do Choice One or Choice Two? Or Choice Three?" Then you're going to say, this one is good for this, this is good for that, and the other is good for other. And this is what is wrong with one, and with two, and with three.

Then, you're going to go and what you're going to have to do—you're going to have to feel it out. Now how do you feel it out if fear is your god? What are you feeling with, then? Through a lot of fear, you are feeling something that you're supposed to do that is good for you?

That is why it gets convoluted. In the process of creativity, sometimes you've got to baby yourself. Maybe you've got to have a friend come into your house and sit around while you create. Maybe you've got to play music. Maybe you've got to drink a few cups of coffee and get very energized. Maybe you got to go into the ocean.

Maybe you got to get up and dance to happy music. Maybe you need to eat something to bring a little smile to your face—something sweet, eh? Whatever you gotta do to get to that place of creation, then do it. Maybe you got to wear the right kinda clothes. Nothing wrong with that. Do what you need to do. Move yourself to start the flow and keep going.

Then, let yourself create. Sometimes you are going to get something that looks so good right at the beginning, and sometimes you spend a long time trying to create something and it gets worse and worse, and that makes you more and more depressed because you begin to lose the innocence because you begin to wonder what is going to happen with this creation? Who is going to buy it, who is going to support it, where is it going go? And so you begin self-sabotage, and that becomes an endless cycle. You know the cycle.

Maybe you want to write something that's funny, but it's not so funny — it becomes darker. Then we say to go with that. You don't know what is going to come out of you. Do not think you know yourself so well; you have so many lifetimes, so much information in the soul, you do not know how or when it is going to come out. You just have to learn how to surrender to let anything come out. When your focus becomes on the quality of your creation, and we don't mean hyper-focused perfectionist; we are talking about relaxed, joyful, energized creation; then you will see more of what you want to see in yourself.

If you are too tired because of so much time spend trying to create something, if you are too disappointed, if you are too mad, this will paralyze you. You will never finish any creation with that energy, and even if somehow you do, you are going to see the quality is not going to be so good. So what do you do to get the creation? You're doing the work to surrender to the magic of life. How do you do that?

You accept, first and foremost, that everything in your life so far has been for you and not against you. You have to believe in this very powerfully, and then let it relax your soul — so that anywhere that you go in this world, and talk to anybody in this world, you understand what it means to create.

And where there were walls, there will be doors.

Bless you.

Chapter 4 — 4th Key

The Key to Humor

November 12th, 2019
Channeling 7:15 pm
Red Eagle Manor, Malibu, California

Charlie Chaplin

Having a sense of humor is one of the keys to physical
and mental health. The positive and powerful energy that
bubbles up from within you when you laugh is a great
healing. This is why they say "Laughter is the best
medicine." And if laughter is the medicine, then what is
the illness? Perhaps it is despair and the tears, both inner
and outer that come from that pain. The pain of longing
for something that has never come, or the pain of longing

for something to return to you that has been lost. Who knows which is worse? I find that the pain for longing for something that has not yet come to you can mean something very powerful, and that is that you long for that feeling because you know it—you know it as a feeling deep within you—and often we seek things on the outside to match that which we know and feel on the inside. And when we feel the inside and the outside matches, in a feeling, then that is bliss.

This equation for happiness is almost foolproof. Almost. And that one small discrepancy that keeps this equation from being perfect is that you still believe there is an "inside" and an "outside" world. You have compartmentalized facts and observations about the outside world, how it runs, what its problems are, it's structures, it's sciences, its artistic expressions, and the consciousness of the people; how they tend to feel about all of these things. I can assure you that a great amount of freedom can be felt when you no longer separate your inner world and the outer world.

It is all your inner world, for everything that you experience results in a feeling, and that feeling shall be one of freedom and delight, interest, curiosity, insight, and growth, or it shall be oppressive and downright depressing. You can lift yourself out of depression. Humor will do this. Humor is natural to you. Babies laugh without ever hearing a joke; they only feel the energy of anything around them, for they are born with all of their senses awoken.

They laugh, seemingly for no reason, but is there? Is a reason for their laughter, perhaps the same reason that you see statues of Buddha laughing? Perhaps the baby and the Buddha both feel the same thing in their round bellies. Perhaps they know something and are realizing something all at the same time. The feeling, growing, and expanding, resulting in even more laughter and light in their eyes.

When a group of people laugh together, the energy is palpable. To be able to turn anger, frustration into laughter— is very powerful alchemy. The alchemy is so powerful that the physical body reacts chemically in very beneficial ways when a person is laughing. Not only are painkillers and endorphins released within the magical body of every human being, but the intelligence is also stirred, activated, and reset in a more peaceful and energized awareness.

Some say to be a funny person, one must know great pain. And this person needs to have processed their pain in such a way that their perspective brings lightness to a heavy situation. And of course, there must be an acceptance and surrender to a larger understanding of existence. Simply put, to not be so afraid of life or death. Some are so afraid of death, they never truly live; and some are so afraid of truly living, that they are the living dead.

But laughter, and a sense of humor can cut through all of that. Haven't you ever laughed until you cried, or until it hurts? What a wonderful pain. What a healing pain, to laugh until it hurts. You can also cry until you are free.
Of course, those tears must be productive and not indulgent. Productive tears are ones where you truly release your pain, and you are having a deeper

understanding of why the painful situations occurred for you, rather than to you, my friend.

I noticed that even animals have a sense of humor. They certainly play, this we have observed whether it is in our own homes with our dogs or cats or bunny rabbits, or whether it is great beasts on the plains of Africa butting heads or rolling around on the fertile land. If there is play amongst the animals in the natural kingdom, does it not make sense that perhaps, naturally, there must be laughter?

Perhaps some of their sounds that we hear are not communications, per se, but laughter! If there is play, I gather there must be laughter. And perhaps there were members of those packs of animals that are considered to be the comedian of the group. Perhaps some of the animals would gather around, when no humans are there, and under the moonlight, stories were told to one another, and the animals would laugh.

I also find it interesting when some people would say, in anger, "Do you think this is a joke?" What a statement to be said in anger! "Do you think it is a joke?" And that is said when someone does not seem to be taking a situation as seriously as another. And so, thinking of it as a joke is an insult, and lacks respect.

I feel that when one jokes, you are showing great respect for life, for knowing that life is eternal; and that if you bring a sense of humor into situations that are troubling, you will ease your pain. And perhaps you will be able to approach a resolution for your problems with more peace.

Being very tense and having internal chaos is not a very good recipe for wise decisions. A lighter sense of being is better for you. My own childhood was quite painful. My only solace was to sing or dance for me to put food on the table and roofs above our heads. As the years went by, the food became fancier, as well as the roofs. And my artistic expression became more layered.

And yet, I feel more truthful. More authentic, to what I naturally felt about life; that life is beautiful. That smiles are the most important thing you can ever wear. I have heard that your expression is the most important thing that you will ever wear, and I find it to be beautifully true. I know it is nearly impossible to laugh when you are in the throes of your pain, but my friend, at some point you must be kind to yourself.

You must stop hurting yourself. To sink deeper into agony is not the way. You shall not find peace there. The journey continues. You are an eternal being, and though you see yourself as this gender or ethnicity, or age, or cultural background, you are more than this. This is but one costume, but one play.

There are many more seasons and many more plays, and many more characters you shall play. Interestingly enough, they shall all be you. Do not get so accustomed to this person you think you are in the mirror. More than likely, it is your first time being this.

The soul travels through many lifetimes. Many stages.
For some, laughter is a way to avoid an uncomfortable, awkward social interaction. Many laugh when they are nervous or uncomfortable. They use it as a shield to

protect themselves from some anticipated harm. I have great compassion for those people. I sincerely understand that there must be some great pain in the past, some deep hurts, abuses of various kinds perhaps; that have resulted in this self-protective reaction. To laugh nervously or incessantly.

Isn't it curious that when one laughs, with great energy and volume, it is very similar to one crying with equal force? Both are releases, aren't they? Is the human being simple or complex? Perhaps you will feel it is both. But many inventors know that to create a simple device, one that is easy to use by all, requires a great command of complexities. One must consider many, many possible outcomes when inventing something that should be simple and easy to use.

One may even regard a car as a simple vehicle. One pedal is to go forward, another to brake, and the wheel to turn. Very simple concept, and great complexities behind it to make it real. Is the reverse true? Can something that seems to be very complex actually be very simple?
Perhaps; it is like the tide coming in and going out constantly. Perhaps simplicity and complexity are always in motion in the process of life. Many times, you have a complex situation in life, and if someone were to offer you a simple solution, you would remark, "It is not so easy, it is not so simple, this solve."

You have probably said it yourself at times. At some point, the tension builds up so much in trying to figure out what to do, that laughter erupts. Usually, someone interjects with a joke. Humor is a peacemaker, isn't it? Humor tends to break the ice in any social situation. Such wonderful power humor has. If humor is a peacemaker, meaning if two people are in disagreement and something funny happens, or someone interjects humor into the situation, the tension is lessened, and openings happen.

Therefore, peace is more possible. So humor can bring peace to you. Humor is not purely escapism. Oftentimes, humor brings you into the nuance of any situation. Brings you deeper in for more precise understanding. Humor frees you of tension. It is anti-inflammatory. Now, to be able to laugh at oneself, that is a great power. A great quality, and very important for self-healing. Quite frankly. Those who take themselves so seriously are very boring to me. Aren't they to you?

Would it really surprise you if you found out the birds were laughing, or the fish in the sea, or the squirrels in the trees? Or the mountains? Or the stars? Or all the ladybugs? It would be very understandable. For we find god in nature, and if it is easy to accept that there is laughter in nature and you may find god in nature, then one can find an equation here that is far more powerful than the earlier mentioned equation.

The equation here would be that even god is laughing. Not at us, but with us. Perhaps humor itself represents the energy of the great creative force of reality. Whether or not you use the word "god" if you allow the love and intelligence and perspective that humor brings you, if you let that be your god, imagine the experience of life you will have. And the impact you shall have on others. If that matters to you.

I find it quite fascinating that if a person is seen laughing very loudly to themselves, by themselves, for an extended period of time, they would be considered "insane" or "disturbed." But if a person were to cry for an extended period of time by themselves alone, this would not be considered insane. Pain is accepted as normal. Laughter, there must be a reason for that. It is a shame when pain is accepted as the norm and wonderful laughter is suspect. What are they laughing at? Are they laughing at me? Are they hearing voices in their heads?

Have they lost it? Perhaps they have lost it, but the word "it" would have to be more clearly defined. What have they lost if they have lost "it"? Their sense of reality? Or perhaps they have actually come to their senses and begun to see the eternalness of life. Can't you see it? Fear has so much to do with losing your life force, being afraid that your life force will be diminished. The only thing that can be diminished is when you isolate yourself, shut yourself down, succumb to numbness and lose your beautiful sense of humor. Do not let that be your reality, my friends.

In your darkest moments, do your best to find something to bring you laughter. I do not mean this to say that you should not cry or grieve. Those are extremely important parts of a soulful life. But do cry less, and do laugh more. You shall be all the better for it.

And so shall everyone and everything around you, for the energy of humor permeates all of existence. Do not be afraid to laugh. This subject has not been taught in your schools in depth. I hope to bring some energy to this topic in the words that I am communicating to you now.

Please take them with you. Water them as if they were seeds. And if you found them to be already flowering and blooming, as they are on this page, then decorate your life with them. Put them in your hair or in your pocket, or somewhere where you can look at them every day. Tell more jokes. Laugh at others' jokes, even if they are not that funny. It shows that you are relaxing and not taking things too seriously, so much so that it diminishes the joy you feel day-to-day.

Humor is magic. Its magic turns frowns to smiles and softens hearts to love. Shared laughter of the soul transforms and heals and brightens everything. You will see.

Bless you.

Chapter 5 — 5th Key

The Key to Understanding

November 18th, 2019
Channeling 7:10 pm
Red Eagle Manor, Malibu, California

Helen Adams Keller

My name is Helen. What does it mean to understand? Is understanding the same as perception? Physically we are taught that there are five ways to perceive things; five senses. To see it, to hear it, to smell it, to touch it, or to taste it. These are the accepted senses of the human being. Are there more?

The gift of intuition is called "the sixth sense," and that is a kind of seeing, isn't it? That is also a kind of hearing if you think about it, when you feel through your intuition you can actually hear a message from the Universe. There are more than six senses that you sense! There is a sense of justice, a sense of balance, and a sense of self. There is common sense and even more you shall discover.

Some are born without one or several of the physical senses. When one is lacking in these, they are referred to as "handicapped" or "disabled." They are taught to understand the common language of their particular country through other means; their other senses. It is said that when one sense is disabled, then other senses are amplified through the redirection of energy and increased sensitivity.

Communication is happening at all times—everything is alive. Everything is made of pulsating, radiating particles. Even inanimate objects are pulsating atomically. This vibration is what they are made of physically and *psychically* as well.

There is a vibration in that pulsing and vibrating in communication. As you read this, perhaps you are hearing the words. More than likely, it is in your own voice that you hear these words. Or perhaps you can sense the vibration of my own energy speaking through the man who is channeling this material. The masterful well-surrendered channel is an open vehicle for this vibration transmission.

Either way, you are hearing these words, and no sound is occurring in physical terms as you know them. You are hearing, as you read these words silently. You are not smelling these words, nor tasting them, nor touching them.

Pg 71

You are hearing them aloud in your consciousness. Or perhaps you are tasting them! Bon appetit! I wish you hearty digestion of this food for thought.

Give yourself a moment to think about my words. Go into their magic. Animals are communicating to you when they are hungry or would like some affection, or other basic needs. They will let you know somehow when their vocalizations or expressions are not read by their caretakers.

They act out in other ways to get their points across—hopefully for their sakes. Learning to understand basic behaviors from pets requires attention and appropriate sensitivity. Considering the vast amounts of species on the planet, humans are lucky they only take certain animals as pets. I'm not sure a rhino would be interested in urban life!

Infants also communicate their basic needs without an extensive vocabulary. They are pulsating and radiating waves of energy using seemingly elementary sound and gestures. They usually successfully get their basic needs met and points across. Infants live in the energy of authenticity with no layers. They are unashamed of their naked bodies, and do not hold back their tears, laughter or affections.

Theirs is an ever-fascinating world where their gaze can shift from the glorious reality of the room they are in—to the other dimensions of vast magical realms of where they were not so long ago before they were born—perhaps before they were even in their mothers' bellies. They are not clouded by beliefs or disbeliefs. They only believe in Connection.

They are surrendered fully to who and what they are, which is love and magic and eternalness. They are fully flexible in body, mind, and spirit, holding no prejudices nor self-doubt. Their communication is completely authentic to the feelings they are feeling. They expect naturally that others are also like this.

As they grow to learn language, they begin to observe and realize that many of those around them do not speak words that match the vibration a child is feeling that underlies the conversation. Manipulation and self-protection that adults display dawns on them and they must adapt or be crushed. This period of "socialization" as you call it, is problematic and based on self-protection. Mixed messages become more apparent. The senses soon become mistrusted or ignored altogether.

The senses are affected by the emotional state of the person. It is difficult to enjoy a beautiful slice of cake when one is weeping. You may perceive the form of a tree—you may do this with your eyesight, or one of your other physical senses—though I do not recommend tasting the bark of a tree. It is not very pleasant I imagine!

In one of the lifetimes where I was known as Helen, I lacked several physical abilities, and yet I can assure you I did see the tree, and I felt I understood it as a living form of consciousness. To understand something, you must come from a place of stillness, but what does it mean to be still?

It certainly refers to the mind's wheels turning not whether the body is not moving about. In stillness, one is not in the confines of time or space; they are not in the past nor the future.

They are *surrendered*. Sometimes it takes getting the flu to force you to be still or to find great beauty. I recommend finding great beauty everywhere to help you be still. This will require supreme sensitivity and love. You are an emotional being. Which emotions rule you?

Perhaps you experience a range of emotions throughout your day, but there may be an undercurrent of one particular emotion that rules you, that informs every thought and reaction and choice — and of course, therefore, your mood. We would like to say that *that* is what becomes your god. It is not difficult to see what rules you when you simply ask yourself what emotions you most often feel throughout your day.

Is understanding your god an emotion in and of itself? It is a kind of fulfillment, isn't it? You are not taught that understanding is a kind of emotion. Perhaps understanding is linked to compassion, and compassion linked to kindness, and kindness linked to love; so somewhere along this chain, you have likened understanding to an emotion.

Whether you believe it is an emotion or it is not, understanding is a sign of maturity. It is far beyond acceptance. Acceptance itself is a form of tolerance, which is not very friendly. I do not think you would like to be tolerated, or even accepted, simply on the basis of your existence. And no one can do anything about that, therefore they accept you, begrudgingly.

To understand another person's feelings is not very difficult if you take a moment to let go of your own opinions and to release any fears of how their feelings can hurt you.

It is a deep maturity and sign of inner peace which, of course, is a strength, to be able to put one's own emotions aside and truly *hear* another person—to truly see another person—to truly *feel* another person. When you extend your sensitivity fearlessly into the world, understanding will be a great gift; not just for you, but for everyone.

To decode, to decipher and understand you must peacefully tap into whatever capacities you are aware of and opening yourself up to abilities you are not aware of. The native peoples spoke to the plant kingdom in deep meditation to understand what healing medicines were available to them. Their microscope and laboratory were their own divine vessel of Awareness. You have this same ability within you. What information and communications await you to unlock their bounty?

There are battles of countries of individuals, of the animal kingdom, and of the plant kingdom as well. While we cannot stop those battles in the animal and plant kingdom, we certainly can stop the internal battles and understand those with each other. How does one understand oneself? Is the Self-defined by your opinions, your culture, your appearance or your actions?

Or is the self the soulful living spirit that is always communicating its truth in one way or another? Our teachers are very important. There is not a thing that you do that was not shown to you in some manner by someone. Whether you discarded the information or it lifted you like a geyser into the heights of success matters not; for you were given communications of their knowledge, their understanding of whatever it is they have taught to you.

It is a wonderful thing to thank your teachers, to bow your head humbly, that you are given the gift of learning deeper understanding. Even when you were taught negatively charged beliefs and misinformed data, you can open your spectrum wider to receive newer more updated information much like the updates on your mobile devices to make your applications perform better. I marvel at how technology is taught to understand!

Truly understanding a problem or new data leads to solutions; whether it is in mathematics, politics, innovation of any kind, is dependent on understanding. Understanding the principles of reality physically is studied in school. Understanding the basic structure of your reality *emotionally* can be learned anywhere and everywhere. When you have the tools to understand *understanding*, then you are a fully aware being, whether you have your physical senses or not.

The power of your memory is remarkable. At this moment, you can simply think of a favorite food and almost taste it enough so that you may salivate. You may imagine smelling a rose, and its "fragrance" will affect you. That is because your understanding of those experiences of when you did taste that food, or smell that rose petal, locked into your consciousness. It was recorded there as a point of reference.

Learning to still the mind is a similar experience. No matter what you do for recreation, for fun, or for escapism, it is so that you can feel stillness. The great rush you experience in any activity — which gives you excitement, whether it is pleasure-based or fear-based — leads you ultimately to a feeling of surrender and stillness once completed and often during it as well.

When one learns stillness without having to seek it through physical means, wonderful things happen; firstly, that you yourself are more at peace. Secondly, you will find new joy in doing the things that interest you, free of expectation or needing to get something out of it. You begin to create for creation's sake, as you did when you were a child.

The urge to create was so natural and great to you that you did not even need to wait for a piece of paper to draw upon. You would use whatever was there, whether it was the floor, or your hand, or your face, or the wall; nothing could stop your expression and the sheer joy of that connection.

How do you understand a piece of art? If you cannot see, you can still experience a statue; use your hands and feel it. Food can be understood in a different way, simply by smelling it. Imagine if you could take the time to smell food for a bit, deeply and peacefully, before you take a bite, to let its communication speak to you. Your body will begin the process of digestion as it understands the codes of the scent of the food and instantly begins to prepare itself for proper assimilation of its nutrients.

When you have a greater understanding, you will enjoy more things. You will understand why you like it. Understanding is beyond economic classes; one who is a wine connoisseur is not more sophisticated than a homeless person sifting through discarded items, searching for either their breakfast or something to clothe themselves with. Those who understand deeper meanings can explain and teach others.

It is why you have had many teachers in your life, but only some you consider great; now mind you, perhaps

you did not have the understanding to recognize greatness in some of your other teachers.

If you learn to understand more, you will feel more love. You will feel more good feelings, even when you see things that are painful; you will go beyond the pain and find wisdom for yourself. You will find the gratitude for your ability to even be present to situations in life that require your understanding. If you surrender to understanding, you are a master.

To understand, one must be sensitive. One must surrender to their sensitivity. To most, sensitivity is not regarded as a strength, and yet, you admire sensitive artists, sensitive healers, and protect sensitive documents. You cannot create great things without sensitivity.

Are you still trying to understand love, or are you trying to understand people's personal journey while experiencing love? Is it love that really confuses you, or are you troubled by the stumbling and messiness that is often experienced when one is in love?

Love is everything. One may say, "love is everything to me," meaning love, whether it is familial or romantic, is of great importance in one's life. That is not what we mean when we say to you, "love is everything." We mean that love is your *key* to everything. When love is not present, look at what happens to a human being or a plant or an animal, or even your car. Or your city's streets. They deteriorate and either die in neglect or lash out.

you are attuned to and surrender to this kind of
you'll be able to have deep understanding of
ıving conflicts and problems. You will learn how to
rehabilitate rather than to punish, and from this an
entirely new sense of reality shall flood your senses.When
I struggled as a young girl, I did not understand how to
navigate my body or my emotions in a soundless, dark
environment. My path was to surrender to what I could
feel—and through feeling— I began to understand.

Great wise teachers have said, "The entire universe is at
your fingertips," and this was certainly true for me. Even
if you do not have fingertips, the magnificent energy that
you are expands beyond your physical limits and is
capable of feeling the loving force of all that is.

When you experience understanding, Oneness awakens
you. Isn't Oneness what you are all seeking? A Oneness
of humanity, free of conflict and lack?

You seek and create togetherness. Many religions have
taught that there is one god, but what is meant is that
Oneness is god, and if you let Oneness become your god,
you will understand everything and everyone, including
yourself.

Bless you.

Chapter 6 — 6th Key

The Key to Change

November 24th, 2019
Channeling 8:00 am
Red Eagle Manor, Malibu, California

Riz Mirza

It's early morning on a Sunday. I opened the front door of our house and looked at the ocean, which is across the street. It's been so hot lately, even in November; it's funny because I've lived in Southern California for so many years and a part of me still expects it to be chilly around Thanksgiving because of all my formative years in New York City. So it never really feels like Autumn to me until there's at least a chill in the air—and *that*, I mostly only I find in the morning breeze by the beach at this time of year here. Everything is very pastel and quiet and I could hear the waves crashing, although I can't see them.

I didn't plan on channeling today, but here we are. I'm back in my bedroom after breathing in that sweet air. I felt a Guide calling me inside. I think the message began when I started thinking about how much has changed since I was a child from growing up in the deep urban neighborhoods of the Bronx and going to high school surrounded by skyscrapers and subways.

All of that stimulation had its own beautiful noise and a city with very defined seasons, but the second half of my life has been here, surrounded by blue sky and blue water and a lot of light. I think the next chapter is going to be about change in some way, riding the waves of it.

So I'm going to close my eyes—actually, they've been closed this whole time, but I'm going to go in deeper now —because it's time.

Phineas Quimby.

My name is Phineas, and I come to you in this remarkable and curious manner to speak of change. What is the key to understanding change? Musicians change keys, and the music and melody shift to a different vibration. This modulation, this lowering or raising of a key in music— is a dynamic way to expand the experience of the message permeating the music. To change the mood, the musical key is changed.

Some people say to make a change is to "shift gears." They liken their life experience to that of a vehicle's capabilities and movement: each gear having a different calibration of tension within the structure of the vehicle, according to the range of speed that the vehicle is to travel.

One may change the font when writing documents on a computer. The font being changed would then represent a change implemented to express something different. If one is writing in lowercase letters and changes to uppercase, it is to emphasize the point. If one changes volume when speaking, it is also the same. You change your clothes to align with whatever activity you are going to partake in, whether it is athletic or social. There are changes that are perceived to be internal and changes that are observed to be external.

How does change occur? What forces are at play? Of course, we are referring to change that is noticed, and that, of course, is dependent upon the sensitivity of the observer and whether they want to look for changes or not. Some scientists claim that a molecule behaves in a certain way only when it is observed.

There are times when there are changes within you that you do not realize, but others bring to your attention. Sometimes one is too close to something or someone to notice a change; haven't you seen your friends' children after some time, and you are amazed as to how much they've grown? The parent is usually surprised, for they have not noticed the dramatic change in growth.

To find peace and comfort in change and it does not necessarily depend on whether the change is pleasurable or painful. If you are poor and suddenly become rich, though it may excite you with the possibilities that financial wealth can offer, you may still feel like a fish out of water. Your choices still may reflect a poor mindset. You may begin to purchase things, unaware that they are symbolic; more of your lack of understanding of money than your command of it.

For those who long for intimate relationships, and then manifest a romantic connection often stumble through the deep ocean of all that intimacy brings. Coming from loneliness, one's perspective emotionally becomes the filter to all that they experience while loving or trying to love the other person—and while receiving and trying to receive love from the other person. All of this is change from what it was before.

You would do well for yourself to master navigating change. What is the key to this? What is the key to change? Quite frankly, it is that *you must change to change*. Evolution certainly is change, isn't it? When you evolve, you are changing. You are growing. You are adapting to a changing environment. An environment that is also evolving.

When a plant dies, is it evolving? The process involves it drying up and withering, hunching over, perhaps breaking off and falling into the soil, or bugs eating it. Of course, it shall grow again if the conditions are conducive for that. Let us say that it does not grow again. Has it actually died? You already know from your scientific education that matter, physical matter, cannot be destroyed: it can only change its form.

Matter is alive, isn't it? We are not diving into minutia here. We are here to become crystal clear about the eternalness of change, growth, and evolution: not just from the idea of self, but as the nature of all of reality.

These teachings do not need to be "integrated" into your life. Forget integration. Everything is already One. You cannot integrate anything if it is already One; meaning, if there is only Oneness between everything and reality, then what you call "integration" is *actually* you accepting this, surrendering to this, and thriving from this—and helping others to do the same. And, contrary to what others have told you, the universe *does* revolve around you. Isn't that something?

"No matter where you go, there you are," as the old saying goes—and that means that all of the universe is perceived from where you are—your beliefs about it. Look around you, it is all revolving around you.

Whether you think of something that is happening in your close circles of relationships or the world at large, the emotional state you feel is your universe, you are constantly encountering your perspective. What they were trying to teach you by saying the world doesn't revolve around you was to become more peaceful in interaction and caring with others. Still, the saying is a funny one.

So, as all of reality is indeed revolving around you, and assuming that you accept everything is One, then how *does* change occur? Until now, perhaps you have believed in different forces causing change, or perhaps now you are beginning to see the futility of such thinking. Perhaps change is an aspect, an omnipresent quality of the very nature of reality. This frightens many, for they feel they will lose what they have if everything is always changing. They define change as the probability of losing things they cherish. We understand this. You shall not lose what you have—you shall actually begin to see more clearly what you have and that appreciation brings fullness to your life.

As you surrender to the everlasting nature of change, a new feeling of powerful flow shall dawn through your entire being. You shall not be swept away by it, now you shall be One with it. In fact, you shall become very present and still within it. Your thoughts will not be scattered. Your god will not be fear or worry.

You will begin to understand the meaning of the word **reverence**.

Reverence contains within it the feeling of respect, but also of awe, and sacredness. Humility is a feeling one has when one has reverence. When you are experiencing a change in your life that frightens you, remember to breathe deeply as much as you can. Perhaps take a moment to do it now. There is no rush in you needing to understand or receive this transmission. You may come back to it as much as you like and read one sentence at a time and breathe it in with not only your lungs but your spirit.

Some change can happen within you in an instant, and you shall feel it as such; that is a very quick flash of awakening. It is very powerful and can last you for the rest of your life. And some change brews throughout your system like a time-release capsule, giving you bits of what you need to move you through moments of your life. There is no such thing as stagnancy. You may perceive or feel that you are stagnant. During this period, energy is building up within you. The information that you have gathered from your experiences is germinating and getting ready to sprout.

The Spirit Guides have spoken about the *butterfly* time and time again. When the caterpillar becomes the butterfly, has it changed or has it simply become more itself? The old saying, "The more you change, the more you stay the same"—what does it mean? It means this; that the more you change, the more you *discover* yourself.

And so, with regards to the beautiful butterfly and its transformation, we would say that of course it has changed, and of course, it has not changed. Our wish for you is that you change so much that you may become unrecognizable to yourself and simultaneously—finally—become recognizable to yourself.

The very nature of your physical life as a human being is a testament to the validity of change as law. At this very moment, your body is changing. Every cell in your body is aware of its own existence. If you do not believe that to be true, what is your logic behind that? Without going into it too deeply at the moment—for that is not our trajectory here—consciousness is all there is. Everything is conscious. Whether you categorize what you see as sentient beings versus inanimate objects, that is up to you.

Let us return to speaking of change. We can tell you to not be afraid of change. Remind yourself of this advice:

let yourself surrender to the understanding that change is always to help you understand yourself better.

Even if you think the change you are going through is not for the better, you can raise your spiritual force and energy by choosing a more powerful stand. Every moment is changing, so all that is needed is for you to not resist.

Resistance, of course, is rooted in fear. Perhaps you have seen the videos of animals who were raised in captivity and then they are returned to their natural habitat, the cage is opened in the jungle, and the animal does not trust it. They only know one place as their home, and every fiber of their blessed animal instinct is telling them to stay in their cage. One would think that their animal instinct would say, "Hallelujah, we are home!" That glorious moment will take some time.

When you watch those animals looking at the jungle or forest, taking in all of that information through their physical senses with a combination of wonderment, unfamiliarity, strange familiarity, and utter terror all at once, perhaps you can relate to it when you are going through change.

Change will always offer you a deeper understanding of home; home—not as a physical place—but as the acceptance and settling into your peace. And so, the animal begins to put one foot outside of the cage with all senses on alert for any danger. That foot feels the ground, its temperature, its texture; and makes very fast decisions about either leaning into the step or to step back. The senses begin to awaken.

The smell of the plants, the feeling it carries in the breeze, stirs the soul. In that moment, the entire world is changing for that animal. The uncertainty of how or where its next meal shall come from begins to fade. The excitement of exploration and discovery begins to take over you. A sense of freedom that was never even imagined before begins to spread through you. There will be much to learn, and there will be ample opportunity for you to display what you have learned already.

The animal would discover just how gifted they are physically, mentally, spiritually. They'll activate dormant strengths and uncover their own uniqueness.

When change happens, let it excite you deeply, *spiritually*. This excitement may not always be a happy feeling. We recommend you breathe deeply throughout it. As you adjust, you will have more peace and less anxiety about change. This will enable you to understand the sacredness of what you are experiencing and how it is *for* you, rather than *against* you. Like the animal that has been set free from captivity, you'll surrender to the changes birthing within you, the changes manifesting around you, and a very potent and peaceful bliss shall be yours.

What does it mean to change with the times? It is also said that times change. Does time change? Certainly, if you live by the clock, time changes, doesn't it? You began to read this chapter at a "different" time other than now. But it was "now" when you began reading and it is still "now" as you move forward reading this sentence.

Perhaps you yourself have begun to change consciously since you began to read this chapter. You agree that you have something you call time. You have created one o'clock and two o'clock and three o'clock so that you may organize your experiences as a society; otherwise, there is no need for any concept of time.

When you are an infant, you are an infant. You shall change into a toddler, and an adolescent, and a teenager, and a young adult, and an adult, and then middle-aged, and then a senior citizen. But you are still *you* throughout all of it, aren't you? And then, when you die, you shall change form again—and still, you shall be *you*. So what does it mean to change with the times? Is it necessary to change with the times? Are you separate from "the times?"

Separation from anything simply means whether you resist something or you flow with it—there are things you shall refuse to flow with. Let us say you are against something politically; actually, you are still flowing with it, for you are reacting to it, and now you are part of that entire movement. If you physically attack someone or physically embrace someone, even if they resist it, they are still part of the interaction. This cannot be avoided. They are part of the creation of it. They are part of the change.

Life feels best when you do not resist and you begin to see the magic of what you are experiencing. My friend, this would require a great shift, and—yes, I shall say it— a great *change* in your core belief system. We have said it before and we shall remind you again: your experience of life shall change when you change your core beliefs about life.

So, this would mean that you are the power of change in your personal reality: you can choose how you feel. This would not be a superficial change, this would be a change at the very "source code" programming of you. When you change the source code and when you change the operating system—you will change the entire experience.

If you believe the world is a dangerous place, you shall experience it as such. Perhaps you would feel it ignorant to believe it is a 100% safe place. That would depend on what you define as safety. If you do not fear your death in any manner, then you are safe, aren't you?

For you fear nothing—for some, death should be put off as far as possible. Whatever the belief is at your core, you shall feel the emotions that that particular belief brings you. How you feel is ultimately your reality. And if you can change how you feel, then your reality shall change.

We do not mean change your perspective; those words are tepid and quite lame. They lack robustness, juiciness, fire, thunder, and starlight! Why would you choose such boring words as perspective or insight? This kind of change is beyond the marrow of your bones—it is beyond your cells—*it is the source of all of it.*

You have been through enough to simply resign yourself to positive affirmations or New Age fashions! The raw authenticity of the fire of your eternal being is what you seek. It is what is waiting for you at all times, even at this moment underneath your surface. *That* is where we are speaking to—inside of you. Receive it now, and feel the change. Have you ever looked into a kaleidoscope? As you turn it, it changes, and somehow it stays the same. As it unfolds in shapes and colors and darkness and light, you can either surrender and delight in it, or resist.

Like a skilled surfer waiting for the next beautiful wave, you can come alive and feel the vibration in the waters of your life and let go of all the fears of drowning. Learning the nature of the ocean, you can work with it, and you may ride with the wave; in freedom, and balance, and beauty, and excitement. And as the currents and force of the wave that brings you to shore, you may dive safely into the water, knowing it shall carry you and support you. It will be exhilarating. You can then breathe in the air deeply, and do it again and again.

Don't forget that it can be fun. Imagine saying to yourself, "change is fun." Change is fun. Let that expand within your consciousness. Let it be a sweet taste upon your tongue when you say it. And let there be a twinkle in your eye as others watch you say it to yourself or to them. And perhaps even then, they will change — all the more fun for you. The more the merrier.

Bless you.

Chapter 7 — 7th Key

The Key to Healing

November 26th, 2019
Channeling 9:00 am
Red Eagle Manor, Malibu, California

Riz Mirza

Sometimes, when I'm doing something random during my day, something where I'm not paying too much attention, I will hear a name in my head. The name usually is one I don't know or just a first name which I cannot place.

This morning, when I was stirring my tea and looking for my phone, I heard the name "Diana." That name usually makes me think of the Goddess Diana or Princess Di. At this point in my life, doing something as unusual as trance channeling, I've come to accept that this entire reality is one big mystery; maybe Princess Diana was the Goddess Diana. Maybe they're the same soul. Maybe there are several people who are the same soul. Maybe our romantic partners are part of the same Oversoul as us; maybe that's what a Twin Flame is.

I consider myself very open. I study the nature of belief, and how it creates our reality, and how it informs our reactions to what we experience. Some people can easily accept it if you channel an angel, but it's harder for them to accept if you channel a known personality—someone in recent history on Earth. There's no point in debating any of that now, I'm here to share directly with you what I experience as a trance channel.

I always ask people, do you want to live in a world with Spirit Guides, or a world without Spirit Guides? Because no amount of proof will be enough if you don't believe and don't want to believe.

If you want to believe, then believe. If you don't, then don't. Maybe in ten years I'll be looking back and thinking, "I wasn't as open as I thought I was." What difference does that make anyway? We're always growing.

So I feel the energy of Diana right now, and I have great reverence for both identities that this could possibly be. It feels beautiful. As I close my eyes, and I begin my deep breathing, and I just surrender to the message, I think that's what it's about really; as the old saying goes, "Just listen to the message; don't worry about the messenger." But wow, her energy is so royal and yet a warrior too.

Diana

I am Diana. What does it mean to heal? Where there is healing there are wounds. How do we describe a wound? Wounds are painful, emotional or physical.

Physical wounds can happen even if a person is numb in that part of their body. Some external force strikes or pierces a body and changes it. This shock tears into what it hits, changing it structurally. If the wound is physical, the pain receptors send a message to the brain that danger is present, and to take necessary action to protect itself. Even if the body is numb, and a wound occurs, the body immediately processes this and begins to heal itself. The physiological process of responding to the wound is immediate. It is not emotionally driven. It is the built-in mechanism of the reality of a physical body.

We are born with regenerative powers. Scars are the body's signs that it is healing, or has healed a wound. To be battle-scarred emotionally means that you have been through a lot. As you study the idea that all things happen *for* you—because your sole purpose (and your soul's purpose) is to continue to grow, evolve, and unfold into more and more of yourself—you will encounter many opportunities to understand healing more deeply.

Part of the reason we choose to communicate with you in this way is that for all of eternity, we have been One. There are many parts as to why one does anything, aren't there? Why does the body heal? One may simply say, it is the natural instinct of survival that makes it do so. Is death a part of healing? We know that we need to heal from the sadness that comes with the death of a loved one. If we are to explore the nature of healing, then we must ask profound and sometimes uncomfortable questions.

If you believe in the eternal validity of the soul, then perhaps even death is the healing of a sick body. The soul leaves behind the body after physical death. The body decays and becomes one with its physical environment, whether it is buried or cremated. The soul, free of the body that was ill, now is in a different kind of body. Some call it the "etheric body" or "heavenly body."

Can this also be said for birth? Is it possible that birth is a healing of some sort? We are getting in very deep now, aren't we? Let us be interested in this exploration; do not be afraid to ponder these things. It is time to stretch the bow of knowledge. If you believe that you have lived many times before, and that all of these past lives were on a journey together to become more and more themselves through lifetimes of triumph and trauma, than perhaps birthing into a new life is the soul's healing.

As you are learning to redefine old concepts, especially in the language that you use internally or externally, you can find healing and new energy in all experiences, no matter their nature; pleasurable or painful. Perhaps for healing to occur, you must say that it is occurring. Perhaps you are the one who is in charge of healing, for you are the receiver of it.

To receive, one must be surrendered and sensitive. One must not let fear be the dominating vibration. When you are ill, it is far better to say "I am healing" than to say, "I am sick." When you repeat that you are sick, you are giving more energy to that, rather than healing. Of course, you must acknowledge that the body is ill—we are, of course, reminding you of the power of your internal dialogue. You must shift your emotional vibration away from the word "sick"—which is tiring, upsetting, and lonesome—to the vibration of "healing"—which is, to put it simply, feeling better so that you can feel better; bringing your focus to pleasurable feelings.

When you laugh, your healing is amplified. When you hug, your healing is amplified. When you are grateful, your healing is amplified. Healing begins with gratitude. I know it is not easy to do this when you are in your trauma: this is something you learn, and it is never too late for self-mastery.

You are born with much more than five senses, and you have the capacity to expand and strengthen and deepen your command of these senses. Healing is also one of your senses. It is automatic; and then, it is also programmable by you. As you lessen the fearful reactive mind, you will awaken the proactive transformative healing mind. You will begin to see the opportunity in everything rather than the so-called circumstances.

Bringing to life this new awareness is built into your system. It can never leave you. You yourself are regeneration personified. You are eternal. You cannot be destroyed. You will only change your form. And your consciousness will expand throughout all of this.

Do not be afraid. Do not be caught up in the dramatic stories of life or how those whom you loved died. Decide very powerfully for yourself that they are in the fullness of their life force and expression and are with you. Decide this for yourself, stay open and sensitive, and you shall begin to feel your loved ones with you. You shall feel them as if they are the ground beneath your feet and the wild blue sky above your head and the breeze that caresses you unexpectedly. Breathe into all of this, for all of this Knowing is a healing.

Let us explore the idea of wounds. Certainly, you wish to avoid wounds; that is natural. And for the most part, I recommend it. You need not learn your lessons only through painful experiences. Oftentimes we are programmed to see growth coming from painful experiences by our elders.

Their beliefs and harshness of the world are matched by the unfolding of harsh experiences. In a way, it is almost as if they are looking for these proofs to validate this troubling belief. You will always find evidence for the beliefs you hold. Your freedom shall come when you choose beliefs that are insightful and open and can bring you greater wisdom and peace throughout any experience.

If your nature is the essence of regeneration, as we share this perspective with you, then perhaps wounds are not really wounds at all. Perhaps wounds are as natural to the nature of life as pleasure. Perhaps wounds are necessary to activate you. This is certainly true in the case of the physical body when it first bleeds; perhaps a child injures their knee from a fall and there is a minor cut. The immune system expands its functioning and heals the wound for the very first time.

This has happened to all of us. Many will say that emotional wounds do far more damage to the being than physical ones. Many walk with a limp if their healing was not complete from an accident years ago. Some cannot live happily or function as a productive partner in a relationship because of old wounds that were not addressed deeply enough to heal properly. Some become better after being hurt: some take their pain and dive deeply into why they manifested these painful experiences. And through that work, they emerge even more peaceful, open, and bright.

Healing must be complete. Complete healing would also have a spirit of freedom in it. What does this mean? It means that you are no longer a slave to the effects of how you used to react to pain. When you calm your reactive mind and use your wisdom to understand your situations, healing begins instantaneously.

How does it begin? Is healing energy a dormant force that exists, waiting for you when it is needed? Can this be tapped into so that it can flow through everything that you do?

You have known some who have surrendered to love. And it seems that everything that they do is healing; they have surrendered to this endless force. And it shows up in how they look at you, how they react, the food that they make, the conversations and tones they have, and in the reactions of those around them who feel it.

You have this capacity as well; do not resist it. You resist it because you are paying more attention to the pain again rather than the healing force. You will have to stop being mad about things in order to feel this energy. If you wish to heal yourself or others, anger cannot be the fuel.

Anger has fear in it, and the fear is based upon suspected harm. And now you are suddenly back, focusing on the pain and the harm. In order to heal yourself or others, you must surrender to the feelings of love. That is the nature of what you are. There are many who study healing modalities; we are referring to those modalities that are currently considered "metaphysical" or "New Age traditions."

It is interesting, to say the least, that most New Age traditions are of the oldest ages known to humankind. There are newer modalities that are transmitted and received by people who share them and master them. There will always be more and more unique and delightful ways of healing.

When you surrender to love as the essence of healing, then anything can be a healing modality. For it is the energy of love that is being transmitted. If you are searching for a way to be a healer, it is not so much the particular modality that you study, but to use that modality to help you surrender to the love that you are — and everyone else is as well.

It is said that words can hurt and other words can heal. That can be a bit problematic if you expect the person who has hurt you with their words to be the person who shall heal you with their words. This is a misunderstanding of personal power. If a person tells you that they hate you, you can receive that as hurtful; or, since you have been studying the nature of emotions and how they occur, you may translate the "I hate you," to meaning "I am hurt and I feel you are the cause."

The entire process can be considered healing from the painful words expressed towards you, and your understanding and definition of the meaning, the source, the essence of those words. You see, healing is truly up to you in any situation. When you understand why you have called in painful experiences, and you remove blame or victimhood, whether you are blaming anyone else or yourself, you will open up the field of your awareness to receive the teaching of the pain. The teaching is not to punish you; rather, it is to help you expand and discover more of who you are.

You will change your life when you regard your pain as sacred: not in a fragile sense, but as a reminder that you are on an endless path of experience. If you surrender to seeing your path, your entire existence—whether you believe only in this lifetime or many lifetimes—as endless, then you may finally relax into your being.

When you change your core belief from needing pain or fear to propel you into further growth to a new belief that there is magic within everything you experience, painful or pleasurable, then you will be free.

You will experience stillness and be able to receive more and more. You will no longer see tragedies as tragedies. You may still feel pain from what has occurred in the past, but you will have a more soulful and peaceful spirit. What is the alternative? If you spin out at the unfairness of the world, it shall not help you. You must heal that frantic energy, for it will undermine all of your efforts to assist others. You must be unafraid to die to truly live. You must understand wounds to truly heal.

Give yourself the gift of making love and understanding your god.

Bless you.

Chapter 8 — 8th Key

The Key to Energy

November 27th, 2019
Channeling 10:00 am
Red Eagle Manor, Malibu, California

Riz Mirza

It was raining all night, and there's finally an autumn chill in the air. I especially like channeling on cozy days. When I woke up this morning, I was having visions of what appeared to be electrons and frequencies, different patterns and soft colors and lines glowing in my mind; I've seen those visuals before in different transcendental states. Some people call it sacred geometry. I like that term, because that's exactly what it is—geometrical shapes, and there is this permeating feeling of sacredness as you swim in it.

I was drawn to sit in my game room for this channeling today, surrounded by video games and LED lights glowing in the dark, and a retro arcade machine behind this big oversized black leather gaming couch, where I am reclining with a thick soft blanket wrapping me up and closing my eyes. I love it here.

There is a very low hum from all of these beautiful magical electrical toys around me and I think I know who I am going to receive this next chapter from. I don't know much about him, other than he was and is a visionary from the other side. Maybe he was always on the other side, even when he was in his human form, so I'm taking my deep breaths as I feel him slowly coming closer.

Nikola Tesla

My name is Nikola, and forever shall I be in awe of reality revealing itself with its generous love that I get to discover, no matter where I focus. My current state is that I am now one with the Eternal Current. You may surrender to this flow or resist it.

I am a student of energy. On Earth it is called electricity, and there are very telling names we give machines that work with electricity (therefore energy): we have generators that create energy, conductors that transmit that information, transformers to vary levels of output, receivers which make the information perceptible, capacitors to store and release energy and information, outlets, and we wrap wires around cores in transmission of energy.

The two must be wrapped around the same core for the transmission to be received. All of these terms are so relevant when it comes to understanding the energy of life which is emotion. They have a parallel meaning when it comes to the soul. You generate or dissipate energy through your emotions, you store it, release it, translate it into words, expressions of great artistic power and body movements, gestures, dance!

The words that are used in technology naturally shall reveal how we understand ourselves. Our physical bodies are all of these terms in action; when the soul surrenders to the Source, then all things are possible. This would be the greatest logic for you to live by and share. Some refer to it as god by many names. The scientifically—or shall I say, so-called scientifically-minded—refer to it now in some circles as "the Unified Field."

Some believe that the universe was created from an explosion. Spiritual realizations can feel like that as well. And when you have an *awakening*, or a spiritual explosion inside of you, it certainly creates a new universe for you. To surrender to Source, I have realized, is the secret and the reason for everything that we do.

For ultimately, joy is what you seek and live for, and perhaps even die for. Physical reality as you know it, meaning your planet, and all of its inhabitants, is a co-created experience brought to life for you to be all that you are and have always been. The illusion for you may be that you must become something other than you are.

Even when energy is amplified, when the signal is made larger or louder, it is simply opening up to its own ever-widening spectrum of inherent power; meaning the more

you feel you are expanding, the more you are coming into the realization of your eternal self. And through you, more can be transmitted to others.

When you speak negatively to yourselves, that is resistance to the Source. You have the power to resist. This is your blessing, not your curse. You are not cursed because you create your reality, you are blessed *because* of it. For energy to be received, the receiver must be open. To be open, you must let go and be still.

Throughout time, people have yearned to master energy. Energy cannot be seen, for it is the field that gives birth to and permeates all. While frequencies can be measured and devices created to give you a visual representation of its vibration and its velocity, source energy itself cannot be seen. It only shows up as something or through something. It gives birth to form, but the source is formless. You may live your own life this way, free of strict identities, affiliations, dogma, and institutionally-backed philosophies.

You must free your mind to have free energy. Do you know the distance between anything is an illusion? There is no space between anything, for nothing is separate. What I used to perceive as space was *my concept* of emptiness. In my travels beyond human incarnation, I have discovered that there is nothing which is empty and nothing which exists separately from anything else. All of creation is linked. All of creation is an extension of itself.

You will experience rapture and freedom and the absence of fear when you step into this garden of knowledge.

Science has learned—by this, I mean the individuals or teams who work within the fields of the current institutions of scientific study—to transmit information, video, audio, through the air without losing its integrity. Structurally, the signals and bits of information are sent into the air and are received and displayed. You find this commonplace and do not stop to be in wonder of this achievement.

Your own thoughts can be transmitted using non-physical technology. When the bits of information are flying through the air, what force is holding it? Is it possible that the air is supporting those frequencies traveling from a satellite to your phone eventually? Indeed, it is. The information is non-physical, whether it is a song or video footage, it makes no difference once you understand how to transmit information energy. Then, telepathic communication will become more accepted.

With each generation, the masses currently do experience telepathic communication, which you refer to as "vibes." Vibes, of course, are vibration: you can feel the vibes in a room, or even in a conversation through texting on your cellular phones. You are such excellent receivers that you are able to feel emotionally the undertone of a text message.

Your ability to store data within your spirit is remarkable if you choose; you are able to experience a moment from your childhood with all of its details in texture, temperature, and so on. These memories carry resonance, another popular term used in technology. To *resonate*

means that magnetic pulsing waves of energy are rippling outward. You can feel the resonance in a person's voice or their creations—be it a painting or a building or a song.

Life itself is energy—everything is alive and always shall be. The so-called "death" is an illusion.

How do you harness energy? To push through old boundaries and limits, there must be hunger. A *hunger* for a better way leads to innovation. You must not repeat, soullessly and blindly, methods that do not bring you the desired result.

Perhaps you are exhausted from your efforts to feel peaceful and yet energized simultaneously. How do you regenerate your energy? You are a natural generator who holds the key of transformation. Locked away in your fears is the seed of boundless energy. If only you would realize that happiness is not only a choice, but also what you are.

If you were taught, from a young age, some of these understandings and perspectives, imagine how much clarity and sanity would be yours. People fall over themselves doing things in the pursuit of being able to receive more energy—relationships and affection energizing you, creative expression, physical satisfaction, mental stimulation. All offer you energy.

The level of power you get from it is up to you. The sensitivity of your receptors defines the impact. The more sensitive you are, the less stimulation you will need, therefore the less energy expended to receive more energy would be the key. If the massive financial resources of the western world were spent in creating small, powerfully ultra-sensitive solar panels, there would no longer be any energy crisis.

What drains mental energy? Finding fault with everything around you will certainly do that. Some get energy from blame, but this energy is not the best kind, for down the line it shall drain you—like anger. Sadness itself has no energy, really, very little. At least anger has some spark that can light a fire to move your spirit. But again, to make a life fueled by anger will certainly destroy you and others. Make love your source. If existence itself is love, and you have decided this to be true, then you will be open to understanding everything existing as coming from love originally.

This concept might be troubling to you, for you find there is much in the world that is wrong. If you want expansive experiences, you must have expansive thoughts. You may use your energy to effect change in the world in any manner that you like, but to resist the idea that at the root of everything is love—meaning the energy which creates everything is the energy of love, and your resistance to that is what changes the outcome—that resistance does not serve your ultimate purpose, which is to feel boundless love.

As humanity begins a true exploration of reality creation by diving into the spirit in a non-religious way, then the discoveries made within shall inform all of the technologies used to assist humanity. Energies required to build the machines that are there, to reduce the energy expended by the human being.

You have the power to cut yourself off from boundless energy. Simply put, once you master your moods, you will access great rivers of energy; galaxies of limitless energy. This can be the greatest realization of humanity and the human being individually—that the actual regeneration of energy is the surrender to source energy which is limitless, renewable, and sustainable.

There will come a time on the planet when vehicles shall be powered by your emotional energy. The vehicles shall be synergistically and symbiotically one with the driver. It is inevitable. If you believe that you are one with god, it means that the creation is one with the creator. And when you are one with god or Source, then all flows perfectly. Then the same shall be true for the ideas of technical innovation.

In the great field of metaphysical knowledge, energy healing is being explored with great success. Understanding that the human body has a field of energy that can receive healing from another person is growing. While the power of touch has been accepted by the masses, now the power of non-touch—as it is traditionally understood—is revealing exciting possibilities. When you touch with energy, you are still touching; and when you touch with energy, you are simply surrendering to the Oneness that is already there.

Energy healing work is the non-resistance to the omnipresent Source. Not only does the physical human body have a field of energy around it, but it is also itself a field of energy that is revealing itself and expressing itself as bone, cartilage, blood, muscle, skin and therefore, can be healed using telepathic energy.

In metaphysical understanding, disease or illness—including the capacity to contract a disease or place oneself in a situation where there is the possibility of contracting a physical illness—that is birthed from an emotional state or core belief about life and how it works.

If you vehemently believe—or are in fear of—bacteria in the environment, coming from a core belief that the world is dirty and unsanitary, then either you shall have a series of complications and challenges, or you will be frantic in an effort to prevent yourself from ever experiencing that.

Your surrender or resistance controls the power of the flow of energy you experience. This is an emotional state of being that rules energy. From the practice of yoga to sports to thrill-seeking, energy is the prize. The release of energy, the expending of energy, and the creation of new energy; whatever gives you all three of these things is what you are after.

If you are a powerful receiver, you can experience this with anything that you choose, rather than only certain activities, which keeps you in constant pursuit and drains your energy. This is a vicious cycle and is inefficient. This mentality is what prevents the world from a cleaner environment and happier people.

Begin with yourself now. There is a day tomorrow that you shall live. You have separated your life by days, and months, and years even minutes and seconds. In order to organize yourselves, you used the physical environment in which you live—the movements of the celestial bodies, the changing of day to night, and the observation of the seasons—to create a system of organization for your lives. If you were to let go of that whole structure, then tomorrow is today.

This does not mean that you suddenly rush out and try to experience everything. This would be frantic and desperate. Indeed, it has been said that all that exists is the present moment. What I would like to share with you is that it is the eternal present moment, meaning it shall never change; it will always be *now*. This is what we would like to convey to you in much of this book.

You may recalibrate with this new perspective and find all that you seek currently in your educational system. You have the study of physics. It would be a pleasure to see the Study of Non-Physics explored with the same amount of interest and funding. Perhaps it shall never be. Perhaps the study of "non-physics" is always happening, and it is far bigger than any institutional university could ever be.

The study of "non-physics" and metaphysics shall put the Universe back in the word University. It will bring integrity that is a testament to true exploration and leave aggressive mean-spirited "scrutiny" behind. To observe and ponder and experiment and have the unknown *teach you its expanded reality rather than to use past information to mold your observation*s is a true science. If you can learn to use any emotional state and turn it into positive energy, you will be a master.

It will take time and great, great emotional strife to have the revelations necessary for true change. The same is true for society, governments and the phrase "Then there shall be heaven on earth" will be understood more profoundly, that wherever you are can be heaven when Oneness is realized. And perhaps that is what is meant by the unified field or One god. There is but One beauty, that is everything that exists perceived physically or non-physically.

At this very moment, you can send energy to anyone, anywhere; past, present, or future. When you fully realize that the past, present, and future are all one, you will have the most powerful explosion of love, birthing universes within you—and within others too—and you shall do this endlessly.

And I will be there with you.

Bless you.

Chapter 9 — 9th Key

The Key to Home

November 29th, 2019
Channeling 11:00 am
Red Eagle Manor, Malibu, California

Riz Mirza

I have been laying here for several minutes breathing and beginning the process of letting go of the external world to prepare to channel this last chapter—observing how my body is breathing and releasing any control of how that happens. So I just become the observer of the breath and how it travels into my body and out. My only focus is to step back from physical awareness, I focus on being un-focused.

My cat is laying across my hips and stomach and I can feel her breathing and her warmth and the size of her small paws. It is a lovely way to channel; I'm interested in her world, and how she sees moving into this new house after so many years in the old ranch on top of the mountain. Now we're across the street from the ocean in a much more modern house.

Cats are so sensitive and aware, it seems they don't like change much-unless there's love. Everything must smell different to her in the air because of the salt, and the water, and the different plants, and the different sounds, but we're here with her—the people that love her, and that she loves—and so she's finding home.

And I feel someone new around me with a message about change and home. Here we go... I'm beginning to hear it rain, and it's sending me further out into that space... of everything and nothingness.

It's a gray day, and I know this woman coming through has seen many gray days, but they were full of hope. The ocean and the sky are gray and glowing today. It's magic. See you later...

Martha Washington

My name is Martha. Throughout time, human beings, and I think even animals, protected their homes. They found some way to secure the entrances with some form of a door and some method of locking it. Have you ever thought about that? That security is a desire and need for all? Safety has always been the defining characteristic of what it means to be home. For most, their childhood homes carry great power and importance.

Those memories—in fact, even if they were not so pleasant—hold many keys. What is it that is so valuable inside the home? Is it the possessions? Many have possessions in their physical houses that are very valuable monetarily, and yet there is a lack of the feeling of home. The feeling of home is a rooted sense of love. The reverse is also true; to have very little material wealth but love, expansive and deep, welcomes you—you feel you belong, and there's no place you'd rather be. You feel nurtured and peaceful.

Some are driven from their homes by political strife, civil unrest, natural disasters; called by opportunities somewhere else, professionally or personally—some are simply driven somewhere new through sheer curiosity and the burning desire to build something new—bigger, better, and freer. This is the nature of the spirit. To ignore it shall only trouble you. To surrender to it begins a great adventure.

The home is considered the sacred space, the dwelling of the physical being and their loved ones. To gather and to nourish their bodies and hearts, to create and share, to learn self-care and to rest their bodies and their minds to dream, and understand, to be home in the world, means *to be at home in yourself*.

When you are at home in yourself, you can be at home in the world. You will learn to nourish yourself anywhere; share, communicate, make memories, create, learn self-care, rest, dream, and understand, no matter where you are. This is how you may find peace as you discover or create a new world. Look upon the horizon with a peaceful gaze, knowing that you shall never reach it. The horizon will always be in the distance. This is a beautiful thing and not something to be frustrated by in your spirit. The horizon represents the endless openness of the journey of life. New horizons simply mean that you are expanding. How beautiful!

Adapting to a new climate in nature—as well as in society—can be challenging if the change is particularly dramatic. The wise person makes peace with this reality, this truth, regarding the process of adapting. Prayer, or meditative practice, is breathing into the present moment without fear. This is true prayer: not asking for anything, but deeply surrendering to seeing the blessings of this moment in your life and in your day. That richness of life that you have longed for will be felt.

If you wish for life to change, to discover or create a new world for yourself, first begin by doing your best to understand your path so far. Do your best to remove self-pity or superfluous praise. Understand that *all* have been in divine perfection thus far, no matter how troubling or unpredictable it may appear. The nature of life brings contrast. Your peace and happiness will depend upon your surrender to Oneness; not despite of contrast, but rather, *because of it*.

You see, *inter*dependence, not independence, is the law of all reality, all universes and dimensions within not only the physical body—as everything works together physiologically—but in all of the external physical reality. Everything works together, even when the lion consumes the zebra, all is in perfect order. By this, I do not mean only the strongest and more aggressive survive. I mean to share with you that while the animal kingdom is considered "wild" it is being as it is designed to be. Some will argue about how a human being is designed and what is "natural" to it. Here we are exploring the reality that all of reality feeds and sustains itself. Grace shall reign when human beings value nurturing as law *rather* than punishment.

This powerful—and perhaps scary—acceptance of this eternal law shall help you when you venture forth into creating a new home or new worlds to be at home in, to not be afraid for very long. While it is natural for fears to be triggered, keep your spiritual eye strong with light. Even the stars are dependent upon you gazing in wonder at them, and the starlight that reaches you, unbeknownst to you, benefits your body, your emotions, and everything around you. There are many things that you cannot perceive that are happening around you which are working with you for your highest good.

What lies beyond the frontier of all that you have known thus far? Does the baby that is about to be born have awareness of what is on the other side of that passageway? Perhaps it does somewhere in its spirit; memories of other lifetimes giving it a mysterious sense of knowing. Does the baby about to be born know fear? Does it wish to be born, or stay in the comfort and nurturing of the world it has known inside the womb that has carried it and made it grow?

There is some overpowering compulsion, a force of nature, where the child knows it must move through that passageway into a wider reality. It also feels the pressure and compulsion of the being that it has been growing within to push it out. This is co-creation. Home birthing home. And once out, the baby sees its creator face-to-face; and after many decades, it shall die and leave its physical body, and go through a passageway into a larger, light-filled reality—and again meet its creator face-to-face. Which place is home then? The eternal creative reality is one with you anywhere and everywhere you bring your focus.

If you find a way to be at home within yourself throughout this endless process and reality, you shall experience the eternal validity of love. When you are told "make yourself at home" it means you are welcome to be comfortable to rest and to nourish yourself without any pressure or pretension. You may truly relax. Can you feel at home in your own body or are you in a constant battle with it? These internal aggressions leave you battle-scarred and weaker. The process of transforming your experience in your body to a happier state begins with gratitude, of course.

Gratitude for where it has brought you to today—at the threshold of a new world you are creating. You must stop hurting yourself to experience being at home in yourself. Some run away from home as children. They leave home for it doesn't feel like home. If and when they return home it is when they sense a change has occurred, that change would be a new commitment to love in the home.

Some flee the countries that they adored until some change forced them to find a new home.

How painful this is. Some have their homelands invaded; throughout history, this seems to be so far an inescapable truth. There will always be room for co-habitation and a shared experience. Many times this has happened more peacefully than others. The battles of the past for feeling at home is deeply personal and has shaped much of the present.

Your instincts for physical survival are innate and automatic. Your emotional survival is far more layered. There is a great difference between surviving and thriving. To be in a new land, to assess and calibrate to the demands of the physical environment—its gifts and its perils—is a natural experience in such an endeavor. But the longing for more freedom powers through it all. One might say that the person longing for freedom is already free when they take action for it.

We must live in this world together. Of this, there is no doubt. And we must live in all future worlds and realities beyond this planet or dimension of experience as one. We are already one. The realization of this is the key. Realization brings implementation. It is not just a thought or concept. Realization means that everything shall become real from it. Self-realization is god-realization, and god-realization is self-realization. All of reality is supporting you, very hard to accept when you are experiencing your struggle for freedom.

Reach into your heart and ask yourself this: *is love your god*? Is it what informs every reaction within you, every creation within you? Even those who speak against you are actually speaking for you. Every obstacle is saying, "You can do it." Every storm is saying, "Either drink this water, capture it so you can drink it later, or be inspired to build a shelter from this rain."

Will you curse it or will you bless it?
Will you bless all that you experience?
Will you consider all that you experience a blessing?

This would be the pioneering spirit in its highest and truest essence of self-mastery and freedom and creation. Every new land, every new experience offers forth to you its resources. When you begin to spend focused and intuitive time observing your environment, you will—in your stillness and relaxed gaze—find the best ways to utilize the resources available to you. The appropriate resources are always with you, and they are linked to the next step, and the next step—the next resource and the next resource, intrinsically—meaning every resource leads you to another.

If you only see scarcity, then scarcity shall be your reality. Each season in nature offers its own gifts, secrets, and resources if you can commit yourself to discover them. At first, your surroundings and resources may seem scarce, but this is where resourcefulness dawns within you. You will discover or birth abilities previously unknown to you: ways to nourish yourself and others, ways to build for yourself or others something new. There is a beautiful humility in this.

Be humble, my friend; be humble. In that humility, there is openness and gratitude. These are the keys for a happy home. You will unlock new magic and rediscover the feeling that you thought was gone. And you shall leave an energetic imprint for all time.

You must let go of where you have been, or where you are, and where you would like to be. If home is where the heart is, then *live from your heart forevermore* and be Free.

Bless you.

ARRIVING LATE 2020

A major inspirational memoir by RIZ MIRZA.

A small band of seekers gathers every week for 7 years at a rustic ranch in the Malibu mountains for a Circle of Light. In search of healing, guidance, and enlightenment, they come to hear the wisdom of RED EAGLE, a Native American message bearer from the 19th century as channeled through **Riz Mirza***, psychic medium. Word spreads quickly among those in the know about Red Eagle's uncanny insights. His powerful words inspire, motivate and bring a lasting sense of peace and calm from those on "the other side..."*

Ten years after those early gatherings, **Riz** *is widely known as the country's premier trance channel, leading two overflow Circles a week plus maintaining an international psychic practice. His in-depth private readings, without the help of his master spirit guides, also change thousands of lives. Read about how he traveled an unusual path to his own destiny... and how you can change yours.*

Please follow Riz for a major book announcement.
Details coming soon.

Made in the USA
Las Vegas, NV
06 September 2022

54789538R00072